Hacktivism and Cyberwars

As global society becomes more and more dependent, politically and economically, on the flow of information, the power of those who can disrupt and manipulate that flow also increases. In *Hacktivism and Cyberwars: Rebels with a cause?* Tim Jordan and Paul A. Taylor provide a detailed history of hacktivism's evolution from early hacking culture to its present-day status as the radical face of online politics. They describe the ways in which hacktivism has re-appropriated hacking techniques to create an innovative new form of political protest. A full explanation is given of the different strands of hacktivism and the 'cyberwars' it has created, ranging from such avant-garde groups as the Electronic Disturbance Theatre to more virtually focused groups labelled 'the digitally correct'. The full social and historical context of hacktivism is portrayed to take into account its position in terms of new social movements, direct action and its contribution to the globalisation debate. This book provides an important corrective flipside to mainstream accounts of e-commerce and broadens the conceptualisation of the Internet to take into full account the other side of the digital divide.

Tim Jordan is a Lecturer in Sociology at the Open University and **Paul A. Taylor** is a Senior Lecturer in the Institute for Communication Studies at the University of Leeds.

Hacktivism and Cyberwars
Rebels with a cause?

Tim Jordan and Paul A. Taylor

LONDON AND NEW YORK

First published 2004
by Routledge
11 New Fetter Lane, London EC4P 4EE

Simultaneously published in the USA and Canada
by Routledge
29 West 35th Street, New York, NY 10001

Routledge is an imprint of the Taylor & Francis Group

© 2004 Tim Jordan and Paul A. Taylor

Typeset in Garamond by
Keystroke, Jacaranda Lodge, Wolverhampton
Printed and bound in Great Britain by
TJ International Ltd, Padstow, Cornwall

British Library Cataloguing in Publication Data
A catalogue record for this book is available from the British Library

Library of Congress Cataloging in Publication Data
A catalog record for this book has been requested

ISBN 0–415–26003–5 (hbk)
ISBN 0–415–26004–3 (pbk)

Contents

Acknowledgements

The first debt of a book on political activists is always to the activists themselves. We talk to, write about and generally enjoy their work, but activists take risks to change the world. Even if we occasionally disagree with them, they have our deepest respect.

Tim would also like to thank all those at *Social Movement Studies: journal of social, cultural and political change*, the folk at Brainstorms, Ray®™, Brian Holmes, John Jordan and, as ever, the great adventurers Kate, Matilda and Joanna.

Paul would also like to thank Ricardo Dominguez and Coco Fusco, Sasah Costanza-Chock and Carmin Karasic for all their help. Lots of love to Lizzie Huang, my fellow soy chicken aficionado – Hen hao, sha gua ben dan, xie, xie! Special love and thanks to Christine and Colin for putting up with Obnox.

1   Hacking and hacktivism

Protest gone electronic

The existence of popular political protest is a mark of all communities; whether it is manifested in spectacular street demonstrations or grey-tinged meetings of local associations. The self-activity of people marks their desire to affect, even control, the spaces and times they live in, even if that means attempting to do so within conditions of no one's choosing. This desire and its always attendant restrictions have become manifest in the spaces and times of virtual lives, both in actions to control cyberspace and actions to affect offline life through cyberspace.

Hacktivism is the emergence of popular political action, of the self-activity of groups of people, in cyberspace. It is a combination of grassroots political protest with computer hacking. Hacktivists operate within the fabric of cyberspace, struggling over what is technologically possible in virtual lives, and reaches out of cyberspace utilising virtual powers to mould offline life. Social movements and popular protest are integral parts of twenty-first-century societies. Hacktivism is activism gone electronic.

While movements to defend cyberspace have existed for some time (Jordan 1999b), the emergence of popular protest within cyberspace – whether about cyberspace or using cyberspace – has not. It is the emergence of virtual direct actions that this book is concerned with. Hacktivism does not mean any politics associated with cyberspace, in which case all politics would be hacktivist as there are very few areas of social and cultural conflict that currently do not touch virtuality in some form or other. Rather, emerging at the end of the twentieth century, hacktivism is a specific social and cultural phenomenon, in which the popular politics of direct action has been translated into virtual realms.

This does not mean that other forms of popular or social movement politics do not exist in cyberspace; it simply means we are focusing on a particular type of cyberspatial politics (Downing 2001; Pickerill 2001; Atton 2002; Meikle 2002). As one pioneer group of hacktivists put it:

> The rules of cultural and political resistance have dramatically changed. The revolution in technology brought about by the rapid development of computer and video has created a new geography of power relations in the first world that could only be imagined as little as twenty years ago: people are reduced to data, surveillance occurs on a global scale, minds are melded to screenal reality, and an authoritarian power emerges that thrives on absence. The new geography is a virtual geography, and the core of political and cultural resistance must assert itself in this electronic space.
>
> (CAE 1994: 3)

This book maps one of the key components of this new geography of power: online direct action or hacktivism. To gain a clearer initial view of hacktivism we must draw out a number of issues.

Hacktivism's sudden and at times shocking appearance resulted from the intersection of three divergent currents: hacking, informational societies and modern social protest and resistance. Below is an outline of the book's structure and content showing how we trace these three currents in order to situate hacktivism within its appropriate political and cultural context, allowing both its novelty and roots to become clearer. Having outlined hacktivism's main influences, it then becomes possible to map its key components and consequences.

Chapter outlines

1 *Hacking and hacktivism*

The present chapter outlines the first fundamental source for hacktivism: the hacking community. Because hacktivism uses computer techniques borrowed from the pre-existing hacker community, it is difficult to identify definitively where hacking ends and hacktivism begins. It is accordingly imperative for our account of hacktivism that we begin in the innards of cyberspace with those who fear no technological boundary; with hackers. The succeeding two chapters will, in turn, deal with the general socio-economic times from which hacktivism emerged and more specifically with the history of protest that hacktivism has drawn upon.

2 *Viral times: vulnerability, uncertainty and ethical ambiguity in the information age*

This chapter explores the general social climate of fear and vulnerability that has accompanied the advent of advanced communication networks. It shows how such phenomena as computer viruses are merely symptomatic of the increased vulnerability felt by developed economies. This is the flip side of their ever-expanding and more complex systems of distribution and transmission that existed prior to 9/11 but are now even more marked. Hacktivism is presented in this context as a form of *virtual politics* that seeks to adapt its mode of dissent to the reality of these complex networks, which it re-imagines as webs to be traversed in a proactive rather than reactive manner.

3 *Hacktivism and the history of protest*

In this chapter the history of protest is sketched in, culminating in an outline of the anti-globalisation movement. This late twentieth- and early twenty-first-century movement forms the key activist context for hacktivism; it is the social movement within which hacktivism arose. To grasp the nature of this movement we fill in the history of popular protest, focusing particularly on changes in the nature of protest following the 1960s. We explore how a newly varied field of popular political activism provided fertile ground for a range of protests and how these accumulated into a wide struggle around the nature of globalisation. Hacktivism in all its incarnations has to be seen in relation to these struggles.

4 *Mass action hacktivism: anti-globalisation and the importance of bad technology*

Mass action hacktivism is one of two main types of online politics that form hacktivism as a whole. Here we meet the invention of electronic civil disobedience in actions that seek to take traditional forms of protest – boycotts, street demonstrations, sit-ins – and reinvent them for the virtual realm. Mass action hacktivism is tied closely to the anti-globalisation movement, with which it has close relations in its support for actions to help, for example, the Zapatistas or to close down World Trade Organisation (WTO) meetings. The paradox emerges that mass action hacktivism seeks legitimation though the support of many people but recreating these bodies in cyberspace, which is inherently a-physical, means rejecting some of the immanent powers of cyberspace. Mass action hacktivism produces limited implementations of cyberspatial powers to ensure its actions reflect a mass politics.

5 *Digitally correct hacktivism: the purity of informational politics*

Digitally correct hacktivism is the second main type of online politics that forms hacktivism. These hacktivists seek to radicalise hacking's original obsessions with information freedom and access by creating tools that ensure cyberspace remains a place where information is freely and securely available. These hacktivists remain close to the hacking community but import concerns about globalisation and its effects on nation-states, particularly where nation-states take up censorship of the Internet. The inherent powers of cyberspace are here built up and relied upon, generating an informational politics that flows with virtuality.

6 *Men in the matrix: informational intimacy*

This chapter builds upon the previous chapter's analysis of digitally correct hacktivism and its privileging of network performance issues over more substantive political concerns. It re-examines the basic nature of hacking in order to shed light on male bias within hacking. It uses this analysis to explore some of the more politically conservative elements of computer-mediated activity in preparation for the following chapter's focus upon the politically radical nature of hacktivism.

7 *The dot.communist manifesto*

In contrast to the partially critical analysis of online political conservatism implied in Chapter 6, this chapter explicitly presents hacktivism as an imaginative, practical response to various theoretical calls for greater engagement with globalising tendencies and processes on their own terrain. Hacktivism is portrayed as an activity that reappropriates the increasingly commercial notion of *performance* and returns an element of drama to the concept. Hacktivism is linked to such notions as *neo-tribes* to suggest that new forms of online co-operation and solidarity may represent the beginnings of a dot.communist manifesto.

With this outline of the book in mind, we can turn to exploring hacktivism. In the first case we must look at the origins of hacktivism and examine its roots. The remainder of this chapter will turn to hacking and its particular attitudes to networked technologies.

Hacking

Initially hacking was predicated upon the imaginative re-appropriation of technology's potential within countercultural and oppositional communities. By the mid-1990s, however, hacking's technological expertise had become, on the one hand, increasingly co-opted by the commercial mentality of the pre-dot.com-bust Internet 'industries' and, on the other hand, was equated largely with illicit, illegal or unwanted computer intrusion (what hackers tended to call 'cracking'). Allowing for disputes over exact times and terminology, hacktivism began at this point, arguably coinciding with the lowest point of hacking's originally uncontested countercultural status.

By the mid-1990s it had become harder to see hacking as counter-cultural or underground as the Internet and personal computer revolution swept first across the developed world and then the globe in an increasingly commercial format. Expanding computer companies hired computer technicians in their thousands, effectively both creating and absorbing the type of computer-trained individuals who previously might have been found only in hacking subcultures. Hacking and hackers had become integral to multi-million dollar businesses; the microserfs had arrived. At the same time, in popular view, hacking gained its overwhelmingly negative association with malicious computer intrusion. The media's interpretation of the word 'hacker' became that of someone who illicitly, even maliciously, took over someone else's computer. The Duke of Edinburgh had his mailbox opened by a hacker, thousands of people's credit card details were downloaded and rumours of bank robberies conducted solely through electronic means were published. Hacking was now synonymous with the notion of someone who used their technical skills to commit computer crime. It is at this moment in hacking's history that hacktivism stirred.

In order to grasp fully this moment, we need first to outline briefly what a 'hack' is and then to introduce the six broad stages hacking has been through before the advent of what we shall term its seventh generation: hacktivists. These accounts are not meant to be exhaustive but rather to delineate fully both hacktivism's roots in hacking and its key distinguishing differences (see Taylor 1999).

The basic element of hacking culture is, unsurprisingly, 'the hack', and, again unsurprisingly given the nature of the neologism, a full understanding of hacktivism requires some familiarity with the concept. The hack did, and still does in various quarters, refer to the performance of a neat programming trick. Despite its connotations of illicit computer break-ins, within hacking circles the hack is more widely defined as an attempt to make use of technology in an original, unorthodox and inventive way. The main bone of contention posed by the criminal forms of hacking (cracking) is the extent to which the ingenuity of the hack should be made subordinate to its legality. While this is a perennial debate, the hack is initially presented here in its widest sense in order to assess any potential commonality that may exist between all its illegal, mischievous and legitimately ingenious forms.

Turkle provides a conceptualisation of the main elements of hacking, which have been confirmed by Taylor's substantial qualitative study (Turkle 1984; Taylor 1999). She conflates the wider definition of illicit hacking with the general mentality of those who see hacking as the manipulation of any technology for unorthodox means. She refers to the hack as being: 'the Holy Grail. It is a concept which exists independently of the computer and can best be presented through an example using another technology complex enough to support its own version of hacking and hackers' (Turkle 1984: 232). The example she uses is that of phone-phreaking[1] and one of its pioneering adherents, John Draper, alias Captain Crunch. The hack, in this instance, refers to such technological stunts as having two phones on a table, talking into one and then hearing your voice in the other after a time-delay in which the original call has been routed around the world. All this is done illicitly and incurring no charge by the relevant telephone companies. Turkle interpreted this type of hack in the following manner:

> Appreciating what made the call around the world a great hack is an exercise in hacker aesthetics. It has the quality of [a] magician's gesture: a truly surprising result produced with ridiculously simple means. Equally important: Crunch had not simply stumbled on

a curiosity. The trick worked because Crunch had acquired an impressive amount of expertise about the telephone system. That is what made the trick a great hack, otherwise it would have been a very minor one. Mastery is of the essence everywhere within hacker culture. Third, the expertise was acquired unofficially and at the expense of a big system. The hacker is a person outside the system who is never excluded by its rules.

(Turkle 1984: 232)

The main characteristics of a hack are that it be simple, masterful and illicit. It is important to note that a key aspect of Turkle's analysis is that the essential attribute of a hack resides in the eclectic pragmatism with which hackers characteristically approach *any* technology. In this sense, hacking has been associated traditionally with such diverse activities as lock-picking and model railway maintenance (and the accompanying tinkering with gadgetry that this involves) (Levy 1984). Hackers themselves refer to the wide range of their potential targets:

In my day to day life, I find myself hacking everything imaginable. I hack traffic lights, pay phones, answering machines, microwave ovens, VCRs, you name it, without even thinking twice. To me hacking is just changing the conditions over and over again until there's a different response. In today's mechanical world, the opportunities for this kind of experimentation are endless.

(Kane 1989: 67–9)

The heterogeneous range of technological targets considered 'hackable' is described by R, a Dutch hacker, who argued that hacking should be defined so that it does not

only pertain to computers but pertains to any field of technology. Like, if you haven't got a kettle to boil water with and you use your coffee machine to boil water with, then that in my mind is a hack. Because you're using the technology in a way that it's not supposed to be used. Now that also pertains to telephones, if you're going to use your telephone to do various things that aren't supposed to be done with a telephone, then that's a hack. If you are going to use your skills as a car mechanic to make your motor do things it's not supposed to be doing, then that's a hack. So, for me it's not only computers it's anything varying from locks, computers, telephones, magnetic cards, you name it.

(R: Utrecht interview)[2]

The three elements Turkle identifies of mastery, simplicity and being illicit create, unsurprisingly, a thrill or what is often described as 'the kick' in creating a hack. The heterogeneity of hacking's targets also fuels the overall feeling of gaining a kick from satisfying the urge of technological curiosity:

in the early days of say the uses of electricity and how to generate it, were first developed, I think Tesla and all the people who were playing with it then were as much hackers as most computer hackers are now, they are playing on the frontier of technology and all those hefty experiments were not only done for science, they were done because they got a kick out of it.

(Gongrijp: Amsterdam interview)

The kick, thus gained, crucially depends upon an element of inventiveness, which serves to distinguish 'true' hacks from those that could be labelled as acts of *Nintendo perseverance*; that is hacks that exhibit large amounts of concentration and dedication, rather than ingenuity (Freedman and Mann 1997).

A further distinction is between original hacks and those that consist of pre-programmed attacks. The latter can be launched, rather than thought out, by what are pejoratively referred to as 'script-kiddies'. Methods of entry may become widely publicised by means of the various branches of the hacker grapevine, such as, electronic and paper-based specialist magazines, the several annual hacker conferences or even word of electronic-mouth. From such sources, hacking 'cook books' of pre-packaged instructions result. Those that predominantly, or exclusively, use such sources of information for the illicit use of a technology would be considered by purists only as hackers in the sense that they fulfil the main requirement of the pejorative definition of hacking; the illicit use of a technology. 'True' hackers, however, are keen to differentiate themselves from such people, by asserting their commitment to the hack roughly as described by Turkle. Using the example of phone-phreaking, Gongrijp illustrates this distinction between a technical and a 'true' hack:

it depends on how you do it, the thing is that you've got your guys that think up these things, they consider the technological elements of a phone-booth, and they think, 'hey, wait a minute, if I do this, this could work', so as an experiment, they cut the wire and it works, now THEY'RE hackers. Okay, so it's been published, so Joe Bloggs reads this and says, 'hey, great, I have to phone my folks up in Australia', so he goes out, cuts the wire, makes phone calls, leaves it regardless. He's a stupid ignoramous, yeah? The second situation is another hacker reads this and thinks, 'hey, this is an idea, let's expand on this'. So what he does is go to a phone box, he cuts the wire, puts a magnetic switch in between, puts the magnetic switch up against the case, closes the door again and whenever he wants to make a free phone call, he puts a magnet on top, makes the wires disconnect, and he has a free phone call, goes away, takes the magnet away and everybody else has to pay. Now he's more of a hacker straight away, it's not a simple black and white thing.

(Gongrijp: Utrecht interview)

The hack is the act hackers perform or the act they like to believe they perform; it is the simplest definition of what hacking means but it is also an idealisation. Hackers, like all of us, find it difficult to perform up to their ideal, and the communities that have sprung up around the hack have developed an array of cultural markers. Having established the nature of hacking's central, distinguishing pursuit, we need to turn to see how this has played out in hacking's history. The hack only exists when performed by hackers, and these hackers rarely, if ever, exist outside their relations to others who form the hacking community. If we can now see what it is that distinguishes hackers, we need to see how their idealisation of themselves has worked within collective relations between hackers. In addition, these communities have gone through significant changes and it is possible to identify up to six different, and frequently overlapping, communities whose common roots lie in their various shades of commitment to the hack. These communities mark the historical stages of the development of hacking; they are precursors to hacktivism and its explicit use of the hack for political purposes.

The hacking community in time and space

It is difficult to schematise the evolution of hacking into neat chronological periods. The following schema of seven generations or groupings of hackers is therefore designed to provide a rough, but hopefully useful, overview of some of the changes that have emerged within the computer underground. It does not, however, adequately reflect the overlaps in time and ethical qualities that exist between the generations so that, for example, there are hackers from all generations who claim to share the central ethos of hacking's first generation. The provisional nature of the schema is further underlined by the fact that definitions of hacking activity are hotly contested both within and without the computer underground and there is considerable blurring of the boundaries between not only 'good' and 'bad' hacking but what constitutes the precise differences between hacking and hacktivism.

The first analyses of hackers identified three intersecting communities, all in some way applying the notion of the 'good hack' to various technological objects (adapted from Levy 1984).

1 *'Original' hackers*: these were the pioneering computer aficionados who emerged in the earliest days of computing. They consistently experimented with the capabilities of large mainframe computers at such US universities as MIT during the 1950s and 1960s.
2 *Hardware hackers*: these were the computer innovators who, beginning in the 1970s, played a key role in the personal computing revolution which served to widely disseminate and dramatically decentralise computing hardware.
3 *Software hackers*: these were innovators who focused more and more on elegant means of changing or creating programs to run on the hardware being hacked up, often by their friends and colleagues the hardware hackers.

Established from the late 1960s to the mid-1970s, these three originating communities intersected and overlapped, such that it would not be surprising if some people fitted all three definitions. Following the emergence of a distinct hacking community, focused mainly on effecting the ideal hack on computer technologies and made complex by interactions between the three just-defined hacker groupings, a number of other generations or sub-communities developed. Again, these should not be taken as completely separate entities but as developing networks of hackers, with individuals often having a place in several camps at once. The first three – original, hardware, software – can be thought of as the path-breaking or 'first generation' hackers who were, almost immediately, followed by new groups and forms of hacking.

As a 'second wave' developed, hackers simultaneously began to be recognised as a subculture. They began to receive significant media attention because, by appearing to be at home with new technologies, they stood out against a social norm of widespread fear of and a sense of disorientation in respect to the changes wrought by the purported information revolution. For example, while not being a de facto hacker organisation, John Perry Barlow and the Electronic Frontier Foundation (EFF) defended several hackers on the basis of the transgression of their civil liberties. The EFF expressed a broad hacker wish to avoid 'a neo-Luddite resentment of digital technology from which little good can come . . . there is a spreading sense of dislocation, and helplessness in the general presence of which no society can expect to remain healthy' (Barlow 1990). Hackers were prototypical denizens of the interstices between old social mores and the cultural implications of new technologies. Hacking was viewed as a postmodern countercultural response to the seemingly inevitable advance of new technology. Hackers were seen to constitute

> a conscious resistance to the domination but not the fact of technological encroachment into all realms of our social existence. The CU [computer underground] represents a reaction against modernism by offering an ironic response to the primacy of technocratic language, the incursion of computers into realms once considered private, the politics of the techno-society, and the sanctity of established civil and state authority. . . . It is this style of playful rebellion, irreverent subversion, and juxtaposition of fantasy with high-tech reality that impels us to interpret the computer underground as a postmodernist culture.
>
> (Meyer and Thomas 1990: 3–4)

This somewhat elevated status afforded to hackers really derives from the hardware and software hackers, whose targets and products began, for the first time, to touch people's everyday lives. The further development of hacking can be described through four inter-related and intersecting groupings.

4   *Hacker/cracker*: from the mid-1980s to the present day both these terms are used to describe a person who illicitly breaks into other people's computer systems, though not always for malicious reasons. The choice of the particular phrase used by a commentator depends

upon his or her perspective. *Hacker* tends to be used by those outside the computer underground, particularly the mass media. *Cracker* is used by those within technology-based groups (both the underground and its institutionally legitimate counterpart, the computer security industry) in an attempt to save the term hacker for its more noble reading of the ingenious manipulation of any technology.

5   *Microserfs*: in Douglas Coupland's novel, the eponymous *Microserfs* (1995) the phrase is used to describe computer programmers who, while exhibiting various aspects of the hacker subculture, nevertheless have become co-opted into the structure of large corporate entities such as Microsoft. Despite, or rather because of, their programming and technical skills, and despite the subjugated connotation of the phrase, microserfs became a stockholding part of the electronic bourgeoisie.

6   *Open source*: the ethic of creating the best possible software led to a broad community devoted to submitting software hacks openly that could then be improved by others. This community connected its concern for the individual hack to a disdain for 'bloated' commercial software and set in chain processes for producing free, elegant (hopefully) and constantly peer-reviewed software. The emergence of Linux as a serious operating system rival to Microsoft's Windows marks this community's appearance as a major player in computing development (Moody 2001).

7   *Hacktivists*: the mid-1990s marked the merging of hacking activity with an overt political stance.

The hacking community, in total, encompasses these seven different generations or groupings, with the possible exception of the founding hackers whose mainframes have gone the way of the diplodocus. Certainly, there are still hardware hackers and software hackers, while the microserfs, crackers and open source movement are all here to stay. To draw out the connection between hacking and politics, since this is the connection which distinguishes hacktivism from other innovative uses of computer technologies, it is now necessary to flesh out the nature of the hacking community. We start by looking briefly at the politics developed by both first and second generation hackers.

Early hacker politics

These were the radical or guerilla hackers, who were destined to give the computer a dramatically new image and a political orientation it could never have gained from Big Blue [IBM] or any of its vassals in the mainstream of the industry. At their hands, information technology would make its closest approach to becoming an instrument of democratic politics.

(Roszak 1986: 138)

In an era of what Roszak calls 'electronic populism', hackers were both instrumental and inspirational figures. This section traces the politicised aspects of the early forms of hacking to illustrate how the activity's inherent values have contributed to the rise of hacktivism through the political formation of the hacking community. As Roszak suggests, within hacking's first generation there were those with relatively radical political motivations who sought to bring computing power to the people. In practice, however, the endgame of such politics tended to be more obscure, given the more immediate and pressing concerns hackers had in obtaining access to systems with a complexity commensurate to their technical knowledge. The ethics of the early generations of hackers stressed the question of unlimited access to computing power and information. For many hackers, both the desire to hack and the attempt to make technology more democratic and accessible were complementary facets of the hacker agenda. This concern, at heart driven by the communities' fascination with performing hacks, was also a double-edged sword. It served to drive, on the one hand, innovative and at times radical views of society while, on the other hand, it pulled hackers toward a fascination with technologies that distanced them from social concerns.

To see some of the initial socially radical impulses of hacking we can start with the Yippies. In May 1971, Abbie Hoffman played a leading role in the establishment of an underground newsletter entitled the *Youth International Party Line* (YIPL). YIPL's first issue strenuously opposed the US government's decision to raise extra revenue for the Vietnam conflict through the taxing of telephone bills. It contained a form to be filled in and sent to the telephone company which stated: 'Because of the brutal and aggressive war the United States is conducting against Vietnam, the amount of federal excise, tax has been deducted from this bill. Paying the tax means helping to pay for outright atrocities, for the murder of innocent women and children' (cited in Bowcott and Hamilton 1990: 49–50). This social radicality did not avoid the lure of the technical hack for too long and in September 1973 YIPL changed its name to the Technological American Party (TAP). Its newsletters provided a raft of detailed technical information, predominantly about how to phone-phreak (obtain free phone calls through the technical manipulation of the phone system) but also on a range of artefacts including burglar alarms, lock-picking, pirate radio and how to illegally alter gas and electric meters.

TAP ceased publication in 1984, but its mantle was taken up in the same year with the launch of the phone-phreak/hacker magazine *2600*, whose ideological stance was immediately indicated by the editor's choice of the pseudonym Emmanuel Goldstein (the name of the protagonist in George Orwell's *1984*). At a similar time in Europe (1981), a German hacker group called the Chaos Computer Club (CCC) was established which directly addressed the political implications of one of the original hacker slogans 'All information wants to be free'. This is a statement of its aims:

> A development into an 'information society' requires a new Human Right of worldwide free communication. The Chaos Club . . . claims a border-ignoring freedom of information which deals with the effects of technologies on human society and individuals. It supports the creation of knowledge and information in this respect.
> (cited in Bowcott and Hamilton 1990: 53)

Anti-corporatist values continued from the earliest hackers and were present in the second generation, as indicated by the names of some of the early start-up companies such as the Itty-Bitty Machine Company (a parody of IBM) and Kentucky Fried Computers (Bowcott and Hamilton 1990: 142). This spirit was not to last, however, and the initial socially liberating and wholesome (hence the choice of the apple brand) potential of such computers as the Apple II eventually succumbed to their status as commodities: 'all the bright possibilities seem so disturbingly compatible with corporate control and commercial exploitation' (Bowcott and Hamilton 1990: 155). The commodification of information proceeded apace with the huge growth in the computer industry, both in communications such as the Internet and other sectors such as gaming and business software. The countercultural hopes pinned upon the computer as a vehicle for anti-establishment values, remained unfulfilled as the spirit of Thomas Paine gave way to the electronic appetite of PacMan. The microserf and hacker/cracker communities exhibited ambivalent political credentials. The early hacker desire to promote free access to computers and information as a means of improving a perceived democratic deficit within society at large, gave way, in time, to more selfish concerns. More attention was now given to access to computers for its own sake and the opportunities for commercial exploitation in an emerging information society.

Anti-authoritarian attitudes within hacking have accordingly been seen less as a form of youthful rebellion and more a sign of a frustrated desire to consume computing resources (Taylor 1999: 53–6), to the extent that one cultural commentator claimed: 'teenage hackers resemble an alienated shopping culture deprived of purchasing opportunities more than a terrorist network' (Ross 1991: 90). Such a pessimistic assessment is vividly developed in Douglas Coupland's 'factional' account of the hacker-type lifestyles of young programmers working at Microsoft's headquarters in Seattle. *Microserfs* identifies 'the first full-scale integration of the corporate realm into the private' (Coupland 1995: 211) with the supplying of shower facilities for workers who wanted to jog during their lunch break being followed by much more significant developments:

> In the 1980s [when] corporate integration punctured the *next* realm of corporate life invasion at 'campuses' like Microsoft and Apple – with the next level of intrusion being that borderline between work and life blurred to the point of unrecognizability. *Give us your entire life or we won't allow you to work on cool projects.* In the 1990s, corporations don't even hire people anymore. People become their own corporations. It was inevitable.
>
> (Coupland 1995: 211, emphasis in original)

The identification of microserfs as the fifth grouping of hackers alongside the sometimes malicious intrusions of crackers, marks the political nadir of the hacker community. Coupland and commentators such as Ross show that the co-option of hacker culture by Microsoft and other corporations has been so successful that corporate-friendly hacking characteristics, such as a programmer's obsession with software coding, had been harnessed to silicon capitalism (Ross 1991: 90). Against this tainting of hacking as either a too optimistic word for newly proletarianised software programming or as a playground for socially regressive crackers, two streams of hacking emerged in the 1990s, or in the case of open source re-emerged. The significance for hacking of the sixth grouping around the open source movement and the seventh in hacktivism is that they mark a retreat from such a pervasive intrusion of commodified values into social life and a concomitant reassertion of more countercultural values.

The open source movement increasingly came into its own by re-establishing the ideal sense of the hack, and this in the hyper-commercialised environment of the Internet boom, pre-dot.com bust. Open source is a complex movement but at its heart its adherents aim to produce elegant pieces of software through the sharing of code to a community which is able to review and improve all hacks. The process is for someone to hack together a piece of code and then to release it to others, who improve, criticise and extend it. Nearly all such software is released free, often with the only licence restrictions being that the software cannot be distributed for profit and any improvements must be made available for others to examine and, in turn, improve (Moody 2001). The now famous Linux operating system, the widely used Apache web-server software and, more recently, the continued development of Netscape browsers in Mozilla are all, in one way or another, open source projects. While open source and its adherents had existed for many years, even perhaps having a claim to be the most direct descendent of the first generation of hackers, open source had also spent many years relevant only to those who were highly technically adept. The purity of its commitment to elegant software hacks often isolated it from vast areas of society which could never hope to use or understand the work of its adherents.

This all gradually changed during the 1990s and early twenty-first century as various open source projects revitalised the hacking community and gave it a relevance far greater than many could have imagined possible in the early 1990s. In particular, the ever-growing influence of Linux has helped to recapture the word hacker for those operating to the highest ideals of the hack. There is no room here to recount fully the story of open source (Moody 2001); it is the concomitant rise of a form of politically motivated Internet-based direct action to which we now turn. However, it is important to note the greater publicity and power of the open source movement with its radical commitment, often directly against the commodification of software, and that this occurred at the same time as the rise of hacktivism. Open source is, in this sense, a highly charged political movement, focusing on information freedom (something we will find in a different way articulated within hacktivism) but its politics often remain buried within lines of code. What was occurring simultaneously was the rise of a grouping of hackers whose politics could never be ignored, overlooked or remain hidden in software code. It is the use of computers for direct actions that forms hacktivism as a distinct community within the hacking world.

Direct action hacktivism

> Given increasing computer prevalence and the fact our political opponents are among the most wired in the world, it is foolish to ignore the computer. Rather, it is important to turn our attention toward the computer, to understand it, and to transform it into an instrument of resistance. For the luddites of the world who resist computers, consider using computers to resist.
>
> (Wray 1998: 1)

Hacktivism has its roots in the swirling currents of hacking. For some fifty years now, technologists outside and inside legitimating institutions have played with computer technologies, trying to generate moments that are masterful, simple and illicit. Through the two generations of hacking and beyond the corporate recuperation of the microserfs and the underground self-obsession of cracking, hacktivism (alongside open source) has emerged to generate a hacktivist community, which this book outlines and explores.

However, there are two other contexts for hacktivism that need to be filled in before we explore more closely the direct actions that make up hacktivism. First, there is the general social and cultural context of the new information or networked society, which we will take up in Chapter 2 through the theme of viral times. Second, there is the history of popular protest and direct action that has been surprisingly joined to hacking in hacktivism (the subject of Chapter 3). Having completed hacktivism's background, we will then turn to detailed analyses of the two main types of direct actions hacktivists undertake: mass actions (Chapter 4) and digitally correct actions (Chapter 5). Finally, having established some of the main forms hacktivism takes, we will turn to its wider social and theoretical significance in Chapters 6, 7 and 8.

The apparently near-total dependence of contemporary national governments and global capitalism on complex communication networks has created room for a deliberately focused political agenda to be added to the pro-systems but anti-authoritarian tendencies that have always existed within hacking. The huge recent growth in the number of such systems of communication networks has simultaneously increased the global commodification process and its vulnerability to dissenting forces. Hacktivism comes from hacking to threaten commodification and state control of information.

2 Viral times

Vulnerability, uncertainty and ethical ambiguity in the information age

Introduction: viral times

> The damage a successful supervirus could do is almost incalculable. 'It would be as if the Millennium Bug has actually done everything it was feared it could do,' said one London-based computer security expert last week. . . . One source close to British intelligence services says MI5 believes both the Basque separatist group ETA and the Kurdish terror organisations have drawn up plans aimed at crashing air traffic control systems through the use of hacking or viruses. Irish Republican terrorists are also thought to have considered similar methods. 'The super-virus is going to happen soon,' the source said. 'There are people out there with that intention. They may coincide their actions with protests against the International Monetary Fund and the World Trade Organisation, just to muddy the water.' Many of the organisations connected with anarchist violence in London number hackers in their ranks.
>
> (Burke and Paton 2000: 19)

The end of the twentieth century was a point of cumulation and recognition that the nature of society had changed. New social and cultural forms, variously described as informational, postmodern, postindustrial, complex, mobile and(/or) networked, had become established. Rather than arguing over whether something new had formed or not, social, political, economic and cultural commentators turned to analysing these forms. It is within these new social and cultural figures that hacktivism emerged; an information obsessed politics for informational times. This chapter will set out this broad social and cultural context. This should not be seen as an analysis of some economic 'base' that truly explains hacktivism. Rather, we explore social, cultural, political and economic trends that both underpin and are formed by hacktivism.

Like all new forms, the social and cultural patterns of the information society do not completely destroy already existing models. Just as feudal aristocracies continued within industrial capitalism, altered to be sure but still existing, so with informational societies both old and new social forms coexist. The drive to profit through the exploitation of labour and the permanent revolution of economic production, so characteristic of industrial societies, remains within informational societies. This drive is reinvented and recreated, yet still exists both in its old industrial forms – such as the massive ship-wrecking yards of India – and in new informational exploitations – such as the huge call centres servicing first world countries with developing world labour.

One way of grasping these continuities and changes is to explore the twenty-first century through the metaphor of what we shall call *viral times*, because this metaphor provides a focus on aspects of information societies relevant to hacktivism. In this chapter we see the way in which, through their creation of conditions that allow information to act in viral-like ways, the complex communication systems of advanced capitalism create lacunae or dark spots where institutional control becomes increasingly difficult. In these dark lacunae hacktivism comes alive. We show how this has facilitated various media alarms and scare stories. These led to early hacker groups becoming stigmatised and marginalised (Taylor 1999) and they continue to colour the present-day public understanding of hacktivism. The notion of viral times, however, also serves to describe the general capitalist environment and its expansive growth, allows us to incorporate the discussion of hacking in Chapter 1, connect it to hacktivism and place all this within the framework of twenty-first-century societies.

Times of the virus

Modern technological times can be described as being increasingly vulnerable to a wide range of viral and other security-transgressing threats to social well-being. Western society has recently experienced such incidents as cyanide-laced Tylenol, the crash of computer systems controlling a major port, glass shards in baby food, benzyne in mineral water, a computer virus that continually rebooted any PC connected to the Internet, chemical poisoning on the Tokyo subway, the Millennium Bug and repeated publicity describing the potential for widespread destruction to technological infrastructures from determined cyber-terrorists. A gap seems to have arisen between society's increasing dependence upon complexly networked communication technologies and its ability to maintain and control such technologies. The quote at the beginning of this chapter, taken from a broadsheet newspaper article entitled 'Coming to a Screen near You', indicates the way in which the press have dramatised society's vulnerability to computer security weaknesses by loosely grouping together such disparate phenomena as hacktivists, terrorists and both computer and biological viruses.

Perceptions of technological vulnerability exist within a wider social climate of insecurity that is fuelled by the contemporary prominence of a number of viral infections ranging from Aids and Ebola, to the scarcely detectable prions in BSE-infected meat. This is a culturally receptive environment for the concerns that have accompanied the advent of IT-based superviruses and which are reflected in the following sample of newspaper headlines:

Love Bug Virus Creates Worldwide Chaos, *The Guardian*, 5 May 2000 (p. 1)

New 'Love Bug' Viruses Threaten More Havoc, *The Independent*, 6 May 2000 (p. 12)

Supervirus Threatens IT Meltdown, *The Observer*, 7 May 2000 (p. 2)

Beware Stealthy 'Sons of Love Bug', *The Independent*, 21 May 2000 (p. 11).

Previously hackers, and now increasingly hacktivists, provided a scapegoat for this feeling of vulnerability as well as a target for fears of the unknown and 'the other' that had prospered during the Cold War and which are now recycled in terms of information warfare. Ironically, given the abstract nature of cyberspace, perceptions of what could be termed techno-vulnerability are often expressed with recourse to body-based forms of expression.

The form and content of more lurid stories like *Time*'s infamous story, 'Invasion of the Data Snatches' (September 1988), fully displayed the continuity of the media scare with those historical fears about bodily invasion, individual and national, that are endemic to the paranoid style of American political culture [and] the paranoid, strategic mode of Defense Department rhetoric established during the Cold War. Each language repertoire is obsessed with hostile threats to bodily and technological immune systems; every event is a ballistic manoeuvre in the game of micro-biological war, where the governing metaphors are indiscriminately drawn from cellular genetics and cybernetics alike.

(Ross 1991: 76)

The breadth of such feelings of vulnerability exist across the political spectrum as illustrated by the following excerpt from an edited collection of articles devoted to providing a predominantly left-wing critique of the values inherent in 'microcybernetic consumerism'.

The disturbing prospect is that opposition to the microcybernetic consumerist dictatorship will then find its only effective location deep underground, in the hands of zealots or fanatics who are content to destroy without bothering to dialogue. And microcyber-netic technology is particularly vulnerable to just such a sort of opposition; as we have seen, hackers generally get caught only when they become brazen; and a determined band of computer nihilists, endowed with patience as well as skill, could even now be ensconced deep in the system, planting their bugs, worms and bombs.

(Ravetz 1996: 52)

The usual levels of media hype that exist around any significant news story, in the case of hacking and hacktivism, have been compounded by the fact that these activities relate, in the eyes of the public, to the recondite area of computing. Exacerbating the process still further is the anonymity and the non-physical nature of these computer-mediated acts. The combination of these factors makes a heady brew for those wishing to sensationalise the issue, and elements of the early hacking community contributed their own brand of rhetoric to the mix with the adoption of colourfully threatening group names such as The Legion of Doom, Bad Ass Mother Fuckers and Toxic Shock.

Pre-existing societal feelings of technological vulnerability may be deliberately exaggerated by those with varying degrees of the hacker mentality, but such hype itself merely reflects more deep-rooted fears about technological change in general.

The tie between information and action has been severed . . . we are glutted with information, drowning in information, we have no control over it, don't know what to do with it . . . we no longer have a coherent conception of ourselves, and our universe, and our relation to one another and our world. We no longer know, as the Middle Ages did, where we come from, and where we are going, or why. That is, we don't know what information is relevant, and what information is irrelevant to our lives . . . our defenses against information glut have broken down; our information immune system is inoperable. We don't know how to reduce it; we don't know how to use it. We suffer from a kind of cultural AIDS.

(Postman 1990: 6)

In this context, the perceived problem with hackers (as we shall see in more detail in Chapter 6) is their over-identification with this informational flood. When their informational intimacy was prototypically path-breaking it was easier to view them, at worst, as mischievous pranksters and, at best, as real-life cyberpunk heroes. As society's dependence on information and its matrices grew, however, the question of how to treat such figures became much more vexed and loaded. This makes the viral nature of modern and postmodern times a significant factor initially for hackers and now for hacktivists.

Co-option and the otaku

We're still not sure what happened to the pirate flag that once flew over Apple Computer's headquarters but we do know that what was once a nerd phenomenon backed by an idealistic belief in the freedom of information became the powerful aphrodisiac behind sexy initial public offerings. Che Guevara with stock options.

(Hawn 1996: 2)

We have seen previously how hackers and their fictional representatives intimately identify and interact with both abstract communication systems and more prosaic artefacts. In addition, at a more metaphorical level, hackers have been accused of identifying too closely with the code of capitalism. Instead of using their technical proficiency in order to control the worst excesses of corporate-driven technological progress and redirecting it to more countercultural ends, they are instead charged with reinforcing its values as their ingenuity is co-opted by corporate concerns.

the hacker cyberculture is not a dropout culture; its disaffiliation from a domestic parent culture is often manifest in activities that answer, directly or indirectly, to the legitimate needs of industrial R and D. For example, this hacker culture celebrates high productivity, maverick forms of creative work energy, and an obsessive identification with on-line endurance (and endorphin highs) – all qualities that are valorised by the entrepreneurial codes of silicon futurism. . . . The values of the white male outlaw are often those of the creative maverick universally prized by entrepreneurial or libertarian individualism . . . teenage hackers resemble an alienated shopping culture deprived of purchasing opportunities more than a terrorist network.

(Ross 1991: 90)

The ambivalence of hackers' claims to be a countercultural force is mirrored in an inherent contradiction of cyberpunk literature. Cyberpunks are presented as anarchic opponents to established corporate power yet the genre is marked by the frequency with which the cyberpunk's human agency is subsumed to the greater ends of their corporate hirers. They fail frequently to redirect corporate power to more humane ends and this is perhaps due to the ultimate conflation of the desire of cyberpunks/hackers and of corporations for technological experimentation. Hackers and cyberpunks only wish to surf the wave of technological innovation, but corporations constantly seek to co-opt that desire for their own ends.

There is . . . a tension in cyberpunk between the military industrial monster that produces technology and the sensibility of the technically skilled individual trained for the high tech machine. . . . Even the peaceful applications of these technologies can be subordinated to commercial imperatives abhorrent to the free thinking cyberpunk. There is a contradiction between the spirit of free enquiry and experiment and the need to keep corporate secrets and make a buck. Cyberpunk is a reflection of this contradiction, on the one hand it is a drop-out culture dedicated to pursuing the dream of freedom through appropriate technology. On the other it is a ready market for new gadgets and a training ground for hip new entrepreneurs with hi-tech toys to market.

(Wark 1992: 3)

A dramatic example of both the alienating and co-opting aspects of hacker behaviour is provided by the phenomenon of the otaku who have various hacker attributes. The phrase is used to describe a Japanese subculture whose members are noticeable by their preference for interacting with machines over people and their penchant for collecting, exchanging or hoarding what for non-otaku would seem trivial information, such as the exact make of socks worn by their favourite pop star. The most publicised otaku to date is Tsutomu Miyazaki who abducted, molested and mutilated in a serial killing spree four pre-teen Tokyo girls. The quality of alienation associated with otaku culture is inadvertantly indicated in one reaction to this case from an otaku seeking to distance Miyazaki from the movement.

> 'Miyazaki was not really even an otaku,' says Taku Hachiro, a 29-year-old otaku and author of Otaku Heaven. . . . 'If he was a real otaku he wouldn't have left the house and driven around looking for victims. That's just not otaku behavior. Because of his case, people still have a bad feeling about us. They shouldn't. They should realize that we are the future – more comfortable with things than people,' Hachiro said. 'That's definitely the direction we're heading as a society.'
>
> (Greenfeld 1993: 4)

Along with this alienated aspect of the otaku is their amenability to co-optation by corporate culture.

> 'The otaku are an underground (subculture), but they are not opposed to the system per se,' observed sociologist and University of Tokyo fellow Volker Grassmuck. . . . 'They change, manipulate and subvert ready-made products, but at the same time they are the apotheosis of consumerism and an ideal workforce for contemporary capitalism'. . . . 'Many of our best workers are what you might call otaku,' explained an ASCII corp. spokesman. 'We have over 2,000 employees in this office and more than 60 percent might call themselves otaku. You couldn't want more commitment.'
>
> (Greenfeld 1993: 3 and 4)

The over-willingness of the otaku to identify with the system represents a danger inherent in hacking's technology-based origins. We will explore the implications of this over-identification in more detail in terms of hacking's *parasitism* in Chapter 6 and throughout the rest of this book we shall see the ways in which hacktivism sets itself up in opposition to it. More pressing to nation-states than the issue of possible over-identification with systems, however, is another worrying aspect of information flood: the issue of cyberterrorism.

Cyberterrorism

> In the hothouse atmosphere of media hype, our favorite nerds blossomed into mythic Hackers: a schizophrenic blend of dangerous criminal and geeky Robin Hood. Chalk it up to an increasingly bi-polar fear and fascination with the expanding computer culture.
>
> (Hawn 1996: 1)

The information age's general atmosphere of uncertainty is manifest in the ambiguous ethical status of some computing activities and society's vacillating responses to the maverick qualities that seem to be at a premium in the hard-to-adapt-to high-tech world of constant change. In the post-Cold War world new security fears increasingly centre around the threat posed by cyberterrorists yet the corollary also exists in the tacit pride felt in one's own electronic cognoscenti.

The Israeli hacker Ehud Tenebaum (aka the Analyser), for example, was accused of being responsible for the 'most systematic and organised attempt ever to penetrate the Pentagon's computer systems' (*The Guardian On-line*, 26 March 1998: 2). While Tenebaum was under house arrest in the Israeli town of Hod Hasharon, US authorities were seeking to use his apprehension as a deterrent to other hackers; to quote US attorney general Janet Reno: 'This arrest should send a message to would-be hackers all over the world that the United States will treat computer intrusions as serious crimes. We will work around the world and in the depths of cyberspace to investigate and prosecute those who attack computer networks' (*The Guardian On-line*, 26 March 1998: 2).

However, Israeli public figures took a much more conciliatory attitude to Tenebaum's activities and their implications: 'If there is a whiff of witch-hunt swirling around Washington, then in Israel Tenebaum's popularity seems to rise by the day. Prime minister Netanyahu's first comment on the affair was that the Analyser is "damn good", before quickly adding that he could be "very dangerous too"' (*The Guardian On-line*, 26 March 1998: 2). Tenebaum's lawyer further argued: '"It appears to me he brought benefit to the Pentagon . . . in essence he came and discovered the Pentagon's coding weaknesses", . . . says Zichroni, adding sardonically that the US authorities should maybe pay Tenebaum for his services' (*The Guardian On-line*, 26 March 1998: 2, 3). Such comments may be interpreted as a lawyer's tongue-in-cheek defence of his client, but they have a deeper significance. For example, they point to the way in which the unethical aspects of Tenebaum's actions are blurred by their potential use to industry and national security. This is illustrated by the fact that he was subsequently asked to appear before the Knesset's committee for science and technology research and development. Just as previous figures in the hacking community have been stigmatised in order to provide a useful embodiment of media-sponsored fears of technology, so hacktivists are now likely to be targeted as scapegoats for fears that have found a fresh focus in the figure of the cyberterrorist. However hacktivists, because they generally propose anti-state agendas, are unlikely to be condoned by their own nations just because they have performed a good hack.

George Smith the editor of the online *Crypt Newsletter*, is mordant in his criticism of the weak investigative qualities consistently illustrated in the press's reporting of cybersecurity issues. He identifies the use of the phrase 'Electronic Pearl Harbour' (EPH) as a particularly good indicator of the likely inaccuracy of any article. He defines EPH as: 'A bromide popularised by Alvin Toffler-types, ex-Cold War generals, assorted corporate windbags and hack journalists. . . . EPH is meant to signify a nebulous electronic doom always looming over U.S. computer networks. . . . It has been seen thousands of times since its first sighting in 1993' (Smith undated website). EPH is a slogan for US 'info-warriors' whose most potent weapon: 'appears to be the burying of the enemy with floods of vague military philosophy, impenetrable jargon, cliches, scenarios, and aphorisms gathered from popular books attributed to Alvin Toffler, Tom Clancey, and Sun Tzu' (Smith 1999: 1). Smith claims that EPH articles tend to have consistently identifiable flaws which serve as accurate indicators of media hype in the field of computer security reporting, including:

> Obsession with hypotheses upon what might happen – not what has happened. Abuse of anonymous sourcing and slavish devotion to secrecy. All EPH stories usually contain a number of 'anonymoids' – from the Pentagon, the White House [etc.]. . . . Paranoid gossip . . . almost any country not United States can be portrayed as taking electronic aim at the American way of life . . . in a kind of modern techno-McCarthyism.
>
> (Smith 1999: 1)

Such faults in reporting and mild paranoia illustrate an increasingly apparent tension of the modern information age: the uneasy nature of the symbiotic relationship that exists between online and offline activity and the complex ethical issues that arise due to the growing adoption of virtual technologies. In the following report, for example, despite the death of an estimated 1,500 civilians from NATO bombing during the Kosovo conflict, US officials seem to place a disproportionate emphasis upon the legal implications of online activity compared to the real-world effects of their offline policies.

> The Pentagon refrained from unleashing an all-out computer attack on Serbia during the Kosovo conflict because the US was worried about the legal implications of launching the world's first 'cyber-war'. . . .The Pentagon's computer hackers had the theoretical capacity to plunder Mr Milosevic's bank accounts or bring Serbia's financial systems to a halt. But US defence officials said the plans were shelved for fear of committing war crimes.
>
> (*The Guardian*, 9 November 2000)

Similarly, the column inches devoted to the new threat of cyber-terrorism seem to be related more to a distorted perspective generated by media sensationalism than any considered evaluation of its importance in the wider scale of things, as is recognised by some commentators. For example, the email bombing by the Internet Black Tigers in 1998 which was directed against Sri Lankan embassies was, in Denning's view 'perhaps the closest thing to cyberterrorism that has occurred so far, but the damage caused by the flood of e-mail . . . pales in comparison to the deaths of 240 people from the physical bombings of the US embassies in Nairobi and Dar es Salaam in August of that year' (Denning 1999: 26). William Church, editor for the Centre for Infrastructural Warfare Studies (CIWARS) underlines this sentiment with his wry observation that: 'considering the routinely deadly attacks committed by the Tigers, if this type of activity distracts them from bombing and killing then CIWARS would like to encourage them, in the name of peace, to do more of this type of terrorist activity' (Denning 1999: 19).

The basic context of all the above examples of ethical and practical ambiguities and confusions resides in the emergence of informational social processes that are simultaneously abstract yet grounded in (some) very real effects. While hacker culture did indeed provide prototypical examples of how to engage with such abstractions, they tended to do so more as an end in itself rather than merely as a means to an end. Hacktivism, in contrast, seeks to engage much more directly with the political implications of informational abstraction and, in keeping with the original notion of 'the hack', seeks to re-engineer systems in order to more fully confront the overarching institutions of twenty-first-century societies.

Virtual politics

Virtual politics . . . should be founded on defying the neoliberal discourse of technology currently being fashioned by the virtual class. It is crucial to ensure that the political genealogy of technology, of virtual reality, of the reality of virtuality, is uncovered by numerous individuals, groups, classes, and new social movements. Indeed, without such excavations, the increasingly institutionalised neoliberal discourse of technology currently being promoted by the virtual class will rapidly become a source of immense social power. This is why concrete, corporeal, and ideological struggles over the nature and meaning of technology are so important in the realm of virtual politics.

(Armitage 1999: 1, 4)

The analytical aftermath of the September 11 World Trade Center tragedy has shone the spotlight even more brightly upon the issue of global commodity culture and its discontents. For example, Benjamin Barber characterises the most significant element of globalisation as the growing conflict between two diametrically opposed, yet nevertheless, inimically related, fundamentalisms: extreme laissez-faire economics and Islamic zealotry, McWorld versus Jihad. 'McWorld' is the phrase Barber uses to describe the 'sterile cultural monism' (Barber 2001: xiii) that results from the unbridled market's insensitivity to the particularities of the local environments into which its commodities are disseminated. 'Jihad' is used to describe the 'raging cultural fundamentalism' (Barber 2001: xiii) that results from keenly felt dissatisfaction with the perceived negative cultural effects of the ubiquitous spread of commodity values.

While seemingly being antagonistic ideologies, Barber points out that both McWorld and Jihad rely upon the qualitatively new level of international interdependence that communication technologies have created and which arguably distinguishes debates about globalisation from the previous subject area of international relations. Osama Bin Laden's heinous acts, for example, made use of the same media communication channels responsible for the spread of the US commodity values to which he objects so vehemently and destructively. In this respect, Bin Laden provides a particularly egregious example of the general technique of reverse engineering against itself a system to which you are opposed. The reverse engineering of global capital is a technique of the new hacktivist anti-corporate movement heavily influenced by its re-appropriation of pre-existing hacking techniques. However, while some conservative commentators have been quick to seize upon this remote similarity of approach to the terrorist attacks of 9/11 by labelling hacktivists as information-terrorists, we argue that hacktivism is an imaginative and defensible attempt to re-appropriate new information technologies for societies' benefit.

At the start of this section, Armitage argued for a 'virtual politics' to compensate for the way in which capitalist values have become inextricably insinuated within new information technologies; hacktivism can be seen as a response to this call. The key significance of hacktivism rests upon the way it confronts head-on Armitage's call for the paradoxical need to affirm the status of the corporeal within virtual politics while adding the constant concern of hackers to defend and extend freedom within incorporeal realms. Hacktivism takes politics infused with concerns about real-world conditions into the abstract heart of contemporary capitalism, while at the same time dragging hacking's traditional politics of information into new, unexpected alliances. Hacktivism is an attempted solution to the problem of carrying out effective political protest against a system that is expanding its global reach in increasingly immaterial forms.

Immaterial capital

> Constant revolutionizing of production, uninterrupted disturbance of all social relations, everlasting uncertainty and agitation, distinguish the bourgeois epoch from all earlier times. All fixed, fast-frozen relationships with their train of venerable ideas and opinions, are swept away, all new-formed ones become obsolete before they can ossify. All that is solid melts into air, all that is holy is profaned.
>
> (Marx and Engels 1972: 476)

In this quotation we can see how long ago Marx identified capitalism's tendency to abstract from material conditions and to plunge all social relations into constant revolution. This immaterial aspect of capitalism first emerged in the industrial revolution, and the spate of information-based technological innovations in recent years are embedded within the same process. What has led to claims that this new revolution is qualitatively different and merits specific attention, however, is the way new information technologies have become crucially and inextricably aligned with social trends. Capitalist values have penetrated into the social environment in unprecedented breadth and with levels of invasiveness that raise qualitatively new social issues. These include the threat to national cultures from the global spread of commodity values (the McWorld effect) and narrowly defeated attempts to exert commercial property rights over such basic material as human DNA. Marx's metaphorical description of capitalism's growing ephemerality is increasingly manifested in the immaterial commodity forms created by the conjunction of information technologies and capitalist markets.

A key component of these new socio-economies is still easily identified in Marxist terms. Marx delineated the origins of capitalism's particularly incorporeal form of value and argued that, in his analysis, the commodity form moves society's focus from use-value to exchange-value. An object's social worth is no longer its practical usefulness, but rather its abstract monetary value in the marketplace, its exchange-value. The significance of the new global information order is that while the initial process of abstraction analysed by Marx still tended to be embodied in physical objects, new forms of informational commodity value have taken the abstract, non-physical element of value to qualitatively new heights. The contrast between the traditional corporeally based form of capitalism and its new cyber-variant is vividly illustrated in the personal account of a computer programmer, Ellen Ullman, and her thoughts about what to do with some New York real estate she and her sister had inherited on her father's death:

> I imagined I really could turn this collection of mortar and bricks into a kind of bond, not a thing but an asset, that I might undo its very realness, convert it into something that will come to me in . . . dustless encrypted, anonymous, secure transactions. . . . It would be money freed of ancient violations and struggling tenants, distilled into a pure stream of bits traversing the continent at

network speed, just a click away – hardly money at all, but some new measure of value: logical, dematerialized, clean

(Ullman 1997: 61)

Ullman reflects the multilayered transformation captured in the notion of viral times. Not only are her thoughts an economic reflection on intensified profit taking, but they also respond to deep cultural anxieties about an existential weightlessness. The very word 'clean', tacked on at the end makes starkly clear the ethical questions of living implied here. It would be a deep mistake to see Marx's prophecies of immaterial values as purely economic, rather there are dimensions here that touch on all our daily lives and our understandings of what our worlds are and should be.

Capitalism's ability to operate simultaneously at both the material and immaterial level has been well documented. We need only gesture here to the current array of economic, cultural, political and sociological texts deeply engaged with notions such as mobilities, networks, flows and so on. All these, some in theoretical and some in detailed empirical ways, document the new society that has come about in the twenty-first century. Further, in these new e-times, business gurus have enthusiastically re-appropriated Marx's account of capitalism's iconoclastic effects while at the same time inverting its ethical and political message, swamping his critical approach with a tsunami of techno-enthusiasm. The continued relevance of Marx's poetically charged analysis and its simultaneous highlighting of capitalism's increasingly immaterial yet destructive form is reflected in such titles as: *The Empty Raincoat*, *The Weightless World*, *Living on Thin Air* and *Being Digital* (Handy 1995; Coyle 1999; Leadbetter 1999; Negroponte 1999). These techno-utopian tracts can even make the language of Marx seem pale, leading to the claim that they represent the 'deranged optimism' and 'corporate salivating' of 'business pornography' (Frank 2001).

The manifest destiny of viral societies

Now capital has wings.

(New York financier Robert A. Johnson cited in Greider 1997)

For how many eons had insurmountable geography impeded man's business? Now the new American race had burst those shackles. Now it could couple its energies in one overarching corporation, one integrated instrument of production whose bounty might grow beyond thwarting.

(Powers 1998: 91)

The phrase 'manifest destiny' was first coined by John L. O'Sullivan as editor of the *United States Magazine and Demographic Review*. He used the term to argue that opposition to the US takeover of Texas from Mexico failed to take into account that 'the fulfillment of our manifest destiny to overspread the continent allotted by Providence for the free development of our yearly multiplying millions' (cited in Brown 1998: 2). Manifest destiny is still a relevant concept when considering the present-day global supremacy of the US corporate model.

One memorable incident, at a meeting of economic policy-makers from the largest industrialized countries that was held in Denver in June 1997, signaled the new mood. President Clinton and Larry Summers, then deputy secretary of the treasury seized the occasion to tell the world about the miraculous new American way. They handed out pairs of cowboy boots and proceeded to entertain the foreigners with what the *Financial Times* called a steady diet of 'effusive self-praise' spiced with occasional 'harsh words . . . for the rigidities of French and European markets'. Don your boots and down with France!

(Frank 2001:7)

This account neatly portrays how the concept of the Wild West works as a trope for US attitudes to globalisation and reflects its dismissive view of those who believe in the importance of protecting cultural resources from the excesses of the free-trade model. The Wild West motif, and its implicit notion of virgin territory to be conquered, encapsulates the view that social and cultural space (like Ullman's previously cited notion of sterile, abstract space) should be subordinate to the requirements of departicularised, abstract capitalism.

This process can be compared to the biological propagation of the virus and is perhaps best encapsulated in the form of the franchise. It is interesting at this point to compare fictional and non-fictional accounts of this process. In the dystopian cyberpunk novel *Snow Crash*, for example, commercial growth is seen as a proliferating force.

The franchise and the virus work in the same principle; what thrives in one place will thrive in another. You just have to find a sufficiently virulent business plan, condense it into a three-ring binder – its DNA – xerox it, and embed it in the fertile lining of a well-travelled highway, preferably one with a left-turn lane. Then the growth will expand until it runs up against its property lines.

(Stephenson 1992: 178)

Stephenson, even with poetic licence, is close to Naomi Klein's similar account of the 'clustering' strategy employed by Starbucks:

Starbucks' policy is drop 'clusters' of outlets already dotted with cafes and espresso bars. . . . Instead of opening a few stores in every city in the world, or even in North America, Starbucks waits until it can blitz an entire area and spread, to quote *Globe and Mail* columnist John Barber, 'like head lice through a kindergarten'.

(Klein 2000: 136)

The Darwinian dystopia described in *Snow Crash* resonates with the real world views of such corporate giants as Ray A. Kroc, the founder of McDonald's, who once said of his business rivals, 'If they were drowning to death, I would put a hose in their mouth' (Schlosser 2001: 41). While this might be viewed as an excessive statement of capitalist competitiveness, evidence remains of the market's inherent insensitivity to local context. This was vividly highlighted by the curator of the Holocaust museum at Dachau who complained about McDonald's distributing leaflets in the car park: 'Welcome to Dachau', said the leaflets, 'and welcome to McDonalds' (Schlosser 2001: 233).

The branding element of advanced capitalism necessarily involves a strong commitment to homogeneity, succinctly described by Theodore Levitt: 'The global corporation operates with resolute constancy – at low relative cost – as if the entire world (or major regions of it) were a single entity; it sells the same things in the same way everywhere. . . . Ancient differences in national tastes or modes of doing business disappear' (cited in Klein 2000: 116). Much anti-globalisation protest objects to this homogenisation and the way in which it extends beyond the heavily branded products of global corporations into the wider urban environment through the formation of what Deleuze terms *espace quelconque* or 'any-space-whatever' (Deleuze 1989). A stark difference between hackers and hacktivists that we explore throughout this book relates to their sharply divergent attitudes to this process of abstraction.

Hackers remain obsessed with a wilful immersion in the abstract environment of computer code whereas hacktivists connect this immateriality to the importance of a social or political rationale, even when an action is co-ordinated in cyberspace or is about cyberspace.

New information technologies, and the e-boom (and the e-bust) premised upon them, are predicated upon departicularised, abstract spaces and flows and are therefore good vehicles for capitalism's abstracting tendencies. Computer code necessarily creates generic models of reality that in the words of progammer Ellen Ullman, which echo Deleuze's notion of *espace quelconque*: 'I begin to wonder if there isn't something in computer systems that is like a surburban development. Both take places – real, particular places – and turn them into anyplace' (Ullman 1997: 80). The lack of rootedness and materiality that these processes tend to create in contemporary businesses leads Ullman to complain of: 'The postmodern company as PC – a shell, a plastic cabinet. Let the people come and go; plug them in, then pull them out' (Ullman 1997: 129).

This section has explored an apparent intensification within capitalism of its tendencies to shift away from the particularities of the local and community in preference for abstract spaces. Klein calls this 'a race towards weightlessness'. We shall see in the next section and through the final part of this book that while hackers and their fictional counterparts, cyberpunks, have enjoyed the race, hacktivists have engaged much more directly with the social consequences of such abstract weightlessness. A defining feature of hacktivism is its willingness to confront the very real, grounded, political problems the race to weightlessness brings in its wake (Klein 2000).

E-commerce as empire

> Along with the global market and global circuits of production has emerged a global order, a new logic and structure of rule – in short, a new form of sovereignty. Empire is the political subject that effectively regulates these global exchanges, the sovereign power that governs the world.
>
> (Hardt and Negri 2000: xi)

The urgency of tone in much anti-globalisation literature and protest is due to a keen awareness of the transnational imperatives of global capitalism that have virally propagated beyond their former confines and into social and cultural realms. Social and commercial boundaries have become increasingly blurred. Awareness of this has fuelled Hardt and Negri's reinterpretation of Foucault's concept of the *biopolitical*: 'In the postmodernization of the global economy, the creation of wealth tends ever more toward what we call biopolitical production, the production of social life itself, in which the economic, the political, and the cultural increasingly, overlap and invest one another' (Hardt and Negri 2000: xiii). An obvious downside of this situation for the critics of capitalism is the way in which more and more aspects of social life become subject to commercial pressures or even simply become commercial in and of themselves. However, simultaneously, the fact that such a process is occurring means that cultural life may become more political as these viral pressures provoke resistance and conflict.

Hardt and Negri, however, identify a potential problem for such resistance. They argue that the nature of global biopolitical forces is such that new forms of social activism are faced with the 'paradox of incommunicability' (Hardt and Negri 2000: 54). They define this paradox as the fact that, despite the rhetoric of the information age, effective communicating about local struggles is made more difficult by the tendency for such events to jump vertically into the global media's attention. A good example of this would be the Tiananmen Square protests which made a huge impact upon global media but achieved little in terms of the desired change within their own local environment. The paradoxical element of this situation stems from the fact that greater media coverage of an event may actually diminish the ability to communicate about political action in more local or horizontal terms.

In contrast to Hardt and Negri's rather pessimistic identification of this 'vertical jump', increasing theoretical attention has been given in recent years to the positive potential opened up by communication technologies for more horizontal modes of communication. In the classic Marxist perspective, whereby capitalism contains the seeds of its own downfall, the ever more efficient circulation of commodities and information also signals greater potential for strategies of resistance. Lash, for example, argues that: 'With the dominance of communication there is a politics of struggle around not accumulation but *circulation*. Manufacturing capitalism privileges production and accumulation, the network society privileges communication and circulation' (Lash 2002: 112). From this new network society, Dyer-Witheford sees new possibilities for protest and the undermining of the status quo: 'the cyberspatial realm . . . increasingly provides a medium both for capitalist control and for the "circulation of struggles" ' (Dyer-Witheford 1999: 13). These writers imply that information capitalism may be faced by a new set of problems if not a web of its own making.

From networks to webs

> The terminals of the network society are static. The bonding, on the other hand, of web weavers with machines is nomadic. They form communities with machines, navigate in cultural worlds attached to machines. These spiders weave not networks, but webs, perhaps electronic webs, undermining and undercutting the networks. Networks need walls. Webs go around the walls, up the walls, hide in the nooks and crannies and corners of where the walls meet. . . . Networks are shiny, new, flawless. Spiders' webs in contrast, attach to abandoned rooms, to disused objects, to the ruins, the disused and discarded objects of capitalist production. Networks are cast more or less in stone, webs are weak, easily destroyed. Networks connect by a utilitarian logic, a logic of instrumental rationality. Webs are tactile, experiential rather than calculating, their reach more ontological than utilitarian.
>
> (Lash 2002: 127)

The search for oppositional potential in existing social conditions is a feature of much theoretical literature. De Certeau (1988) attempts to counter the pervasive domination of society by commodity values by arguing that models for resistant practices can be found in various day-to-day subversions and within the mode of consumption of everyday products. An example of this is the way in which the indigenous Indians of South America only superficially accepted the framework of the Catholic Church imposed upon them by the Spanish colonisers. Beneath their seeming acceptance these indigenous peoples in fact managed to develop various independent practices that kept their traditional values alive. Drawing upon such examples, De Certeau seeks to promote new forms of resistance to the homogeneity and commodification that otherwise prevails within the market system and which can be seen in terms of an overarching social matrix that contains within it digital matrices:

We witness the advent of number. It comes with democracy, the large city, administrations, cybernetics. It is a flexible and continuous mass, woven tight like a fabric with neither rips nor darned patches, a multitude of quantified heroes who lose names and faces as they become the ciphered river of the streets, a mobile language of computations and rationalities that belong to no one.

(De Certeau 1988: v)

De Certeau's description identifies the all-encompassing and circumscribing nature of such a social matrix and the numerate mentality it relies upon is obviously greatly facilitated with the advent of binary-based digital systems.

While De Certeau talks in terms of a cybernetic 'fabric with neither rips nor darned patches', Lash uses similar language, referring in the quotation at the beginning of this section to the 'flawless' nature of utilitarian networks predicated upon instrumental reason. Again, in keeping with the notion of capitalism containing the seeds of its own destruction, critical social resistance can stem from such utilitarian networks. Owing much to Lefebvre's detailed account of the need to reconceptualise space for more autonomous non-capitalist purposes, both Lash and Klein develop the image of the protest web opposed to the instrumental and 'shiny' image of the network (Lefebvre 1991; Klein 2000; Lash 2002). Klein, for example, explicitly develops the comparison of anti-corporate opposition to web-making spiders:

the image strikes me as a fitting one for this Web-age global activism. Logos, by the force of ubiquity, have become the closest thing we have to an international language, recognized and understood in many more places than English. Activists are now free to swing off this web of logos like spy/spiders – trading information about labor practices, chemical spills, animal cruelty and unethical marketing around the world.

(Klein 2000: xx)

In keeping with what we have previously seen as hacking's penchant for re-engineering objects and systems against their initial purposes, Klein's notion of a global web for the better transmission of oppositional practices provides the basis of a strategy to deal with capitalism's confusingly immaterial iconoclasm. It also resonates with Dyer-Witheford's call for anti-capitalist groups to mimic the nomadic flows of capital within the 'global-webs' of commerce (Dyer-Witheford 1999: 143).

This call for a re-appropriation of the global web is increasingly common. Hardt and Negri, for example, forcefully argue that the circulations and flows of global capital need to be counter-populated with the counter-flows of 'the global multitude' (Hardt and Negri 2000: 46). They also use language resonant of the previous quotation from the novel *Snow Crash* and its comparison between corporate growth and viral propagation: 'Rather than thinking of the struggles as relating to one another like links in a chain, it might be better to conceive of them as communicating like a virus that modulates its form to find in each context an adequate host' (Hardt and Negri 2000: 51). Hacktivists can be seen to be part of this 'counter-populating' of 'the global multitude'.

Conclusion

Hacktivists are the marriage of the spirit of the hack and the spirit of protest in the context of viral times. We have explored the past of hacking, we have introduced the metaphoric realities of viral socio-cultural formations, and to complete the context for the emergence of hacktivism we need to turn to popular political activism and its structures as they existed towards the end of the twentieth century. Indeed, in the preceding few pages it has been difficult to keep protest out. We shall find here, centrally, the emergence of an ill-named anti-globalisation movement, whose methods can easily be described as viral and whose targets are often the immateriality, the virus-like nature, of millennial socio-economies.

> We are trapped in a reality constructed by information – mostly, the particular kind of information that is constituted by images. Our existence, both in its routine and more dramatic moments, is created by information just as it depends on it. . . . A society that uses information as its vital resource alters the constitutive structure of experience. . . . The accelerated pace of change, the multiplicity of roles assumed by the individual, the deluge of messages that wash over us expand our cognitive and affective experience to an extent that is unprecedented in human history. . . .The self is no longer firmly pinned to a stable identity; it wavers, staggers, and may crumble.
>
> (Melucci 1996: 1–3)

Melucci places his finger on the centrality of information in our societies. This constant flux and revision touches us in our economic structures – the commodity form – and our personal subjectivities – the selves that waver. Viral societies can be called viral because information acts like a virus and a virus, whether computer or biological, is a form of information. Viral times calls for viral selves. We shall begin to see hacktivists as some of the most self-assured and active of these selves.

3 Hacktivism and the history of protest

Hacktivism in radical protest

At the last minute the Electrohippies mounted an online protest against the World Trade Organisation meeting in 2001 in Doha. They had been moving away from protests against globalisation to concentrate on protesting against the 'war on terrorism' but in response to requests for an online demonstration, felt by many to be particularly important as being physically present in Doha was difficult, they developed an automated means of sending protest emails. To participate in the online demonstration, protesters could visit an ehippies webpage, click on the particular organisation(s) they wished to write to and then approve the auto-generated email. We will discuss in greater length both the Electrohippies Collective and this particular type of protest, but this example allows us to begin with hacktivism and to see perhaps the key context for hacktivism of protest in the twenty-first century, in the ehippies' target: the World Trade Organisation (WTO).

The WTO is one of a number of international bodies that oversee and organise worldwide economic systems. Other such bodies include the World Bank and the International Monetary Fund (IMF). In addition to these organisations, there are a number of regular inter-governmental conferences that contribute to the organisation of international finance and commerce, such as the meetings of the seven (or eight) largest economies in the world known as the G8. In the late twentieth century, these agencies participated in a reconstruction of global commerce in ways that implemented – variably and not without problem and contradiction – a neo-liberal economic regime. Here are some of the organisers and promoters of viral times.

This neo-liberal, as it is generally known, regime can be thought of most simply as an attempt to implement worldwide a restructuring

of economics that favours free trade for corporations over either collectively organised actors – such as trade unions – or state institutions
and state-sponsored programmes – such as national health bodies or
government interventions into economic processes. The claimed worldwide benefit of this would be a rise in economic activity which would,
in turn, lead to increased corporate profits and greater economic health
that would fuel higher standards of living. The opponents of this
programme saw its effects rather differently.

> Neo-liberalism, the doctrine that makes it possible for stupidity
> and cynicism to govern in diverse parts of the earth, does not allow
> participation other than to hold on by disappearing. 'Die as a social
> group, as a culture, and above all as a resistance. Then you can
> be part of modernity,' say the great capitalists, from their seats
> of government, to the indigenous campesinos. These indigenous
> people with their rebellion, their defiance, and their resistance
> irritate the modernizing logic of neomercantilism. It's irritated by
> the anachronism of their existence within the economic and
> political project of globalization, a project that soon discovers that
> poor people, that people in opposition – which is to say the majority
> of the population – are obstacles.
>
> (Marcos 2000: 280–2)

Subcomandante Insurgente Marcos is the leader of the military wing
of the indigenous people's uprising in Mexico, most often referred to
as the Zapatistas. This uprising became public, through a Zapatista
military occupation of four towns in southern Mexico, on the day the
North American Free Trade Agreement (NAFTA) came into effect. This
agreement bound Canada, Mexico and the United States together into
a free trade area. The virus of neo-liberalism was being embedded in
social life in Mexico through this agreement. It brought viral times
seemingly unstoppably to Mexico. But then, in reaction, the Zapatistas
began to fight against this type of society.

What the previous chapter called viral times was carried to the jungles
of Mexico through NAFTA, though the terms globalisation and neo-
liberalism are more commonly employed. We can now turn to the
self-activity of groups protesting against neo-liberal virality to see the
final, key context for hacktivism. This is a context that is most commonly,
though misleadingly, called the 'anti-globalisation movement'. It is
a misleading name because the movement is not anti-globalisation

but anti-neo-liberal-globalisation. This movement, building upon the socialist tradition of Internationalism, in fact favours various forms of globalisation such as cheaper, global communication that allows trade unions to communicate or campaigns to be co-ordinated. What this movement is opposed to is the particular economic globalisation driven by such organisations as the WTO, IMF or the G8. Unfortunately, the movement is stuck with its name, however inappropriate, and from hereon will be referred to as the anti-globalisation movement.

It is this anti-globalisation movement that is the main political context within which hacktivism has emerged. This chapter will trace the emergence of this movement, connecting it to its history and outlining its main constituent parts. Although it should be kept in mind that these were not the only radical politics going on in the world at the time hacktivism emerged nor are they the only politics which have affected hacktivism. Where hacktivism is touched by a politics that is not clearly part of the anti-globalisation movement – for example, the Italian-based hacktivists Netstrike launched an online action protesting against the death penalty in Texas – then this politics will usually be coloured or framed by anti-globalisation politics. For example, the rationale for the Netstrike action highlighted the disproportionate number of people from non-white ethnic groups who suffered the death penalty and explained this with reference to racisms heightened by neo-liberal economic reforms. The anti-globalisation movement and hacktivism have emerged, struggled, failed and won together. In the overarching context of viral times, and born both from hacking and from the anti-globalisation movement of the twenty-first century, hacktivism is perhaps the first, widespread social and political movement of the new millennium.

Social movements old and new: the hinge of the 1970s

Before we consider the anti-globalisation movement of the late 1990s and early 2000s, we will sketch in briefly a slightly broader context for non-institutionalised political conflict. This will note the emergence of many different social movements as the focus of radical political action following the 1960s, as well as trace the different paths of protest in relation to globalisation in the developed, Western or Northern world and the developing, underdeveloped or Southern world.[1] The key moment in these stories is a transition in the nature of radical politics that mirrors a transition in the nature of society. This transition, from the 1960s to 1990s, can be seen in many aspects of society: from welfare state to privatised state; from imperialism to post-colonialism; from letters to email; from broadcasting to narrowcasting; and in the field of resistance to oppression (and crucially for this story), from working-class revolution to new social movements. This transition from one type of society to another at the end of the twentieth century has been touched on already in the outline of viral times and its association with immaterial capitalism. The prior form of capitalist society, most broadly characterised as industrial capitalism, also developed or included a characteristic radical politics.

At its outset, industrialisation was riven by a number of social struggles: most particularly, the suffragette or first wave feminist move-ment, the anti-slavery movement and the working-class or labour movement. Industrial society's history is then marked perhaps most dominantly by the series of communist revolutions and near-revolutions that seemed to threaten the survival of capitalism itself, alongside the gradually attained legitimacy of less radical labour politics in parlia-mentary labour parties and trade unions. The Bolshevik Revolution in Russia and the Chinese Communist Party's accession to power mark most powerfully a period in which it seemed possible – all too possible ruling elites seemed to believe – that the fundamental economic, political and cultural structures of developed societies could be trans-formed utterly. The near-insurrection in Germany, including successful insurrections in parts of Germany, just after the First World War and the general strike in the United Kingdom seem the most dramatic examples of times when a major, industrialised country seemed to teeter on the brink of a communist transformation. Less spectacular but often equally bitter struggles burst into view between the two world wars in nearly all the western nations. The Great Depression heightened the sense of impending doom for capitalism and the rise of such extreme doctrines and social systems as fascist Germany was welcomed in many so-called 'democratic liberal' nations as an answer to and bulwark against communism (Hobsbawm 1988, 1989, 1995).

As the story is now often told, during the Second World War many capitalist countries developed a corporate approach to management of their politics, cultures and economies. The lesson of state-managed wartime economies was applied to the problem of controlling the transgressive potential of the working class, and led to the development of a welfare state which looked after the interests of not just the rich. This development, not just a ruling-class 'trick' but a compromise based on working-class struggle, meant diminishing class struggle through its institutionalisation and management. Trade unions negotiated with employers, increasingly overseen by state agencies whose aim was to ensure the future of capitalism by ensuring that working-class revolt was blunted. Though undoubtedly an idealised view, this story captures much of how working class conflict was perceived in many capitalist countries as the central economic issue.

At the same time as this political settlement, which placed control of class antagonisms as its central principle, the Cold War made an opposition between communism and capitalism the central geo-political divide. Around the world, all political struggles began to be perceived as moments in the grand chess game between the Soviet Union and the United States, each nation symbolising a particular political, cultural and economic form. The effect was to place class as the central political problem. This can be seen in, for example, struggles against colonialism which were often structured by perceptions of their place in the geo-political game. Would a post-revolutionary government be communist? Was each revolution a communist revolution, no matter what it claimed to be? The interventions of the US/Soviet superpowers and their allies into a colonised nation would often be determined by the current state of the Cold War. In addition, many anti-colonial movements involved Marxist elements, often as core parts of their struggle. The obvious example here is the Cuban revolution, which involved significant nationalist elements that, in the post-revolutionary phase and under severe pressure from the United States while also benefiting from support from the Soviet Union, were minimised during the creation of a socialist state. All these struggles tended to re-emphasise the role of class in politics both locally and worldwide.

At the same time, a further subsidiary factor emphasised the centrality of class relations to radical politics. The success of the Soviet Union in the Second World War, along with the strong role some communist parties played in resistance to Nazism, particularly the role the French Communist Party was believed to have played, led many intellectuals into an association with Marxism. This association was accompanied by a blindness to the failures of Eastern bloc social systems, particularly the carceral network of the Gulags. The symbolic figure here is Jean-Paul Sartre, who shifted publicly and volubly from a philosophical existentialism to an activist Marxism (though of his own interpretation) during the 1950s in France, but he was not the only such figure. For a period Marxism played a central role in intellectual life, a role that is still felt today and was not particularly loosened until the 1970s and later. The effect of this was to make class relations, and in particular radical Marxist interpretations of class, central to most socially engaged intellectual life.

Taken together we can see the post-Second World War period as a time in which class politics emerged ever more clearly and strongly as the central framework for all political struggles. This does not mean that all politics in this period is reducible to class, but that all politics developed within the context of class and had to take account of class by defining itself in relation to labour/capital relations and the geo-political opposition between the United States and the USSR. However, by the end of the 1960s, a major shift was taking place in radical popular politics. This was expressed in both the emergence of many new movements and a final paroxysm of radical Marxism. At the activist level, by the 1970s movements had emerged and continued to emerge that did not seem easily reducible to class and which actively resisted and questioned any such reduction. Second wave feminism, gay and lesbian struggles, civil rights struggles (in several places around the world, such as the famed US civil rights movement but also in Northern Ireland and elsewhere), ecological struggles, anti-racist and black power struggles and more, all created environments where the central political problem seemed not necessarily to be class. At the same time, many activists felt the convulsions, particularly of 1968, confirmed the importance of class struggle, especially when such struggles were freed from the dead hands of Soviet influenced communist parties and set about inventing renewed forms of Marxism. The nearness of revolution seemed to many to confirm Marxism and the necessity of heightened class struggle. However, this can now be seen, in retrospect, as the last paroxysm of Marxism. Not that Marxism disappeared, but that its dominance of radical conceptions and organising of class relations and its part in articulating labour/capital as the central political framework began to unravel. Intellectually and politically, by the 1970s the framework for radical, transgressive, non-institutionalised politics was significantly changing. Alain Touraine remembers that the conception of 'social movements' emerged in this context.

> The idea of social movement was conceived, at least in my mind, in opposition to the traditional concept of class conflict. Not opposition in the sense of being reformist. Instead, when we speak about class conflict we refer, basically, to a process of capitalist

development or a process of social and economic crisis in objective terms. When we began speaking, a long time ago now, about social movements, we tried to elaborate a new approach and to pass on the actors' side.

(Touraine 2002: 89)

Increasingly, it was no longer possible simply to apply Marxism, even in its renovated forms, to the struggles that emerged as the 1970s progressed. This should not be understood as a sudden divide but as a process in which many contradictory elements were felt. For example, at a theoretical level one of the most influential currents during the 1970s was Althusserian Marxism, which was an explicit attempt to rediscover the scientific Marx. This theoretical tradition held great influence in its time but now is often both dismissed as being incorrect (despite Althusser's importance to current influential thinkers such as Foucault) and as evidence of the final failure of radical Marxism. Similar attempts were made to connect Marxism to other increasingly influential theories and movements. Two instances here were the efforts to develop a Freudo-Marxism that tried to integrate class struggle and psychoanalysis and the emergence of socialist-feminism that sought to integrate feminism, actively and theoretically, with labour/capital relations (Turkle 1978; Rowbotham *et al.* 1979). All these manoeuvres were part of this final outburst of Marxist thought as the dominant intellectual and activist framework for radical politics.

As each of these concerns reached impasses or were rejected – whether this was the hyper-Marxism of post-1968 French Maoism or the failures to connect radical movements to labour institutions – it became apparent that a new framework of radical politics was coming into existence. This framework integrated the insight at both intellectual and practical levels that each particular movement had to develop its own insights and actions. Social movements from an activist perspective became self-defining. It was no longer possible to assume that a new form of Marxism or, more broadly, a class politics would capture the essential struggles of women, black people, the colonised, different sexualities, greens or any future, as yet undefined, movement. Indeed, often the identification by class politics of the enemy to be a socio-economically defined ruling class meant misunderstanding the oppressors identified by new movements. In the newly emerging struggles those who were identified as benefiting through domination were defined often not as the ruling class but men, white people, colonisers and imperialists, compulsory heterosexuality and over-developers and so on. At the outset two things need to be understood about this newly emerging framework.

First, the new framework is based on the coexistence of many different movements, each of which engages and defines a form of radical struggle. This multiplicity of movements forms the practical and intellectual horizon of radical politics. Second, politics that do emerge must engage with or define themselves in and against this horizon of a multiplicity of struggles. It is not the case that labour politics in general or Marxist-inspired politics in particular disappear. Rather Marxist movements, ideologies or struggles become one among many others. This is important because the 1980s and 1990s saw a dramatic increase in what many see as class struggles. The reaction to the perceived liberalisation of the 1960s and the perceived 'weight' of the corporate or welfare state led in the 1980s and 1990s to programmes of privat-isation, cutbacks, valorisation of markets and so on; all of which have been known collectively as neo-liberalism. Whatever else these policies were, they were certainly part of a right-wing attempt to remould over-developed and global socio-economies in ways that served corporations and capital far more than unions and labour. Such notable struggles as the miners in Britain or the air traffic controllers in the United States marked a sharp change from the state overseeing stable bargains between labour and capital, even if the state leaned rather to capital's side, to the state championing capital's interests. Yet even such a clear class-based struggle, one extended through the 1980s and 1990s into a global programme of economic change discussed in Chapter 2, did not return class politics as the single framework for radicalism. Instead, it reaffirmed the necessity and relevance of class politics to a framework of many movements and struggles. These policies may seem relevant mainly to the Northern or overdeveloped world but they were also implemented on a worldwide basis. This can be seen in two ways.

First, the institutions of international economic governance, such as the International Monetary Fund (IMF), which had been set up as part of the post-Second World War attempt to manage capitalism by avoiding boom and bust, successfully began to insist on free market policies. Governments that received loans from the World Bank or aid from the IMF began to find – what were in the 1970s and 1980s called 'monetarist' and now tend to be called 'neo-liberal' – strings attached. Necessary loans would only be given if a government committed itself to reducing state intervention, reducing barriers to a 'free market' (in many cases this meant destroying trade unions or community organising and opening up to imports) and aiming for greater growth as defined under capitalism. The programmes of monetarist or neo-liberal intervention attempted to write Reaganism and Thatcherism across the world.

Second, shifts in forms of production and culture, underwritten by key developments in information technologies, involved increasing globalisation: these are some of the concrete elements of viral times. Factories were broken down into their functional elements. This meant the elements of production processes that needed large quantities of labour could be shifted around the globe to countries with low wage costs and little labour organisation, usually away from overdeveloped nations. Many countries were persuaded to set up economic zones in which even the meagre labour protection laws of many underdeveloped countries were suspended. The 'four Asian Tigers' and Japan were highlighted as examples of countries that had begun their economic renaissance by taking on large factories using low-paid labour but had then transformed this fragile economic basis into dynamic developed economies. Such arguments have been heard less after the economic collapse of these countries but are still often used. There is also evidence that transnational corporations are increasingly developing ways of bypassing structures which ensure any benefits are gained by the hosting country. The arrival of the monetarism/neo-liberalism virus in the South and developing world has meant the undercutting of local and communal enterprises in favour of global ambitions. These have often led nations into serious debt problems, which further restrain their ability to create equitable social conditions and often, incredibly, further enrich Northern financial institutions.

In terms of culture, the development of widely enhanced global communication has led to a renewed form of cultural imperialism, in which particularly US media have come to dominate. Satellites, Internet, mobile phones and so on have all extended the reach of cultures around the world. This is a contradictory process and is certainly not one-way, as the size of Bollywood and as the ability of the Internet to be used to create 'local' places that reach globally both show. However, it remains the case that local cultures have increasingly come into contact with media produced and distributed around the world. This is as true of Hollywood films as it is of McDonald's food.

These thoughts outline the overall social and cultural context for radical politics in the period from the 1970s to the late 1990s. It was a period of transition in which the previously assumed centres of politics, the previously dominant forms of struggle and ways of defining struggle, began to fall away to be replaced in both North and South. As we have indicated, the social context for this was in part the collapse of the corporate means of negotiating class conflict that was set up post-World War Two. Of course, the second context for this transition was the end of the Cold War and the collapse of 'really existing socialism' in Eastern Europe. This change contributed to the shift of class politics from the centre of radical politics by removing its institutional supports and further delegitimating radical class politics, even if the latter rejections are partly based on a triumphalist set of partial truths told about ex-socialist countries. The end of the Cold War does not completely end socialism and communism; for example Toni Negri, in conjunction first with Felix Guattari and later with Michael Hardt, has been calling for over a decade for a renewed communism for the new millennium (Guattari and Negri 1990; Hardt and Negri 2000). Such attempts to rehabilitate or reinvent such classic terms of class politics as socialism, revolution, class consciousness and so on, however, all suffer from what Stuart Hall notes is 'a problem of coming at the end of a language rather than the beginning: none of the words will work for you any longer!' (Bird and Jordan 1999: 203–4).

The social context for this shift in the frameworks of radical politics is largely set by the revision of the welfare state and the end of the Cold War which lead to the emergence of new global economic and political projects, and this shift poses numerous problems and opportunities. However, this context should not be understood as a determining context for protest because social movements are part of this change. As Doreen Massey argues:

> Surely it's not a question of the capital-labour settlement breaking down *and then* the other movements taking off. . . . Feminism, sexual politics and post-colonial struggles were part of what destabilised the old, all-too-comfortable, consensus. They were part of the *cause* of the breakdown not simply its effect.
>
> (Bird and Jordan 1999: 198)

Radical politics and social movements are intimately tied up within these shifts; they are both cause and caused by broad political, cultural and economic changes. We can now sketch in the movements that, in fact, developed within this pluralistic framework for radical politics. Here we need to break movements down into Northern and Southern or overdeveloped nations and developing nations. While these categories are still overly broad they provide the introduction necessary to understand the emergence of the anti-globalisation movement, which provides the necessary context for the emergence of hacktivism. Finally, we need to discuss these separately from the emergence in the same times of reactionary movements. We will look briefly at these three in turn.

After the 1970s

In the North or overdeveloped nations there were roughly three waves of social movement activism since the 1970s. In the first, a number of widely influential social movements emerged, at the same time that Marxist-inspired groups and official trade unions began to decline in influence. The roll call here is familiar: second wave feminism, movements around sexualities (gay, lesbian, bisexual and transgender movement and the queer movement), black power and anti-racism and ecological struggles. These four seemed to many to be the inheritors of the left, perhaps along with the peace and anti-nuclear movement, but in fact they each reflect a political framework that included the left but was not determined by a left/right axis. The effects of all four were widespread though not unambiguous.

If it would be foolish to claim that any one of these movements was entirely responsible for changes in the social problems they address, it would be equally foolish to think that they had no effect. If we take feminism as an example, we can see it was engaged with changes in family status, with the position of women at work (especially equal opportunities and equal pay), the treatment of women by the welfare state, women's sexuality and more. The point is not that feminism was unilaterally successful and managed to impose conditions on men that redressed all imbalances of power. For instance, since the 1960s we have seen increasing numbers of women at work, but this can involve both a liberation, with some women having access to jobs they were previously denied, and a burden, with some women finding they are now in work and are still expected to carry the main child-rearing role. The same could be said for the other movements noted here, as well as the labour movement which all through this period continued to produce political moments. None of these have achieved 'victory', even if we could know what such a 'victory' might mean, yet all have achieved victories, suffered losses and, most importantly, participated in remaking the political landscape.

During the 1980s, these movements continued. Sometimes parts of them became embedded in institutional politics, for example in the role women have played in various political parties and governments. Sometimes they have continued generating a radical edge, for example in the way parts of the gay, lesbian, bisexual and transgender movement were radicalised in struggles around HIV/AIDs leading into the queer movement. Some believe these movements at times became reduced to a self-interested 'identity' politics that became obsessed with naming in place of 'real' political engagement, though this may have been most significant in the United States and even there perhaps mainly in US universities (Klein 2000; Starr 2000). At the same time, various labour struggles occurred, often as part of the monetarist or neo-liberal-inspired transformation of the corporate or welfare state. This period also saw a growth in the peace and anti-nuclear movement, especially as part of growing Cold War tensions. By the late 1980s, the ecology movement was drawing new strength, at times making unlikely alliances with new cultures of pleasure and party (McKay 1998).

During the early 1990s, these tendencies continued, though of course with national and regional variations. For example, in Italy the framework of Marxism retained greater power than, in particular, in the United States and, to an extent, the United Kingdom. In Italy social movements not based on class struggles were often integrated within or understood in relation to various forms of Marxism. In order to accommodate these struggles the concept of the 'social factory' emerged for some Italian Marxists. This represented an attempt to conceive of all life along the lines of the factory and in this way rendered Marxism relevant to all social struggles. The theoretical stretch needed to make such changes is obvious – can all social life really be understood as being modelled on the factory? – and suggests that even in Italy the hold and coherence of Marxist frameworks were weakening (Wright 2002).

As the 1990s progressed various changes occurred. The peace movement fell away somewhat with the collapse of the Cold War, the ecology movement gained strength, particularly in the United Kingdom within what has been called DiY culture, and other newer movements emerged, for example in the anti-sweatshop movement in the United States (McKay 1998; Jordan 2002). This latter movement came from the realisation that newly globalised production processes meant that the commodities people were buying in the North had been created utilising extremely poorly paid labour, in some cases virtually the equivalent of indentured or slave labour. Here the realisation was dawning that struggles in the overdeveloped world could not be separated from the developing world. The ecology movement played a key role here; its constant investigation of the exploitation of the world's ecologies ensured a focus beyond the developed world. By the mid-1990s, a significant crossover of North and South led to the globalisation movement. First, we will consider two further factors of 1970s–1990s protest: activism in the South and reactionary activism.

In the South or developing world, struggles were generated at many levels. These can, perhaps, be split into three different types. Unlike the successive waves of Northern movements, these types do not refer to time but to types and spaces of struggle. The broad differences between North and South are captured by Corr when discussing squatting:

> Squatting in the United States revolves around political and social counterculture and the destitution of individual homeless persons in the midst of opulence. Squatting in the Third World is a logical reaction of whole classes of people to the concentration of land in the hands of the few.
>
> (Corr 1999: 39)

It is such differences that demand another approach to outlining popular struggles in the South. We should also be clear that these struggles are not necessarily restricted to the South; instead they are often articulated differently between North and South, as Corr claims in relation to squatting. The following categorisations should also not be understood as mutually exclusive, because groups often link to each other, but they attempt to capture the different archetypes of struggle. First, there are urban-based struggles, often connected to universities and student protests. Second, there are insurrectionary and guerrilla movements. Finally, there are indigenous peoples and peasants movements, particularly over land rights. As with previous outlines, these categories only provide the broadest, sketchiest introduction to radical political struggle in these regions, yet they also provide an adequate basis for understanding the forces that underpin the anti-globalisation movement.

Urban struggles, often linked closely to student struggles, occurred throughout the South. During the 1970s to 1990s, processes of urbanisation continued, even becoming heightened as more and more people were drawn from rural to urban areas. These processes often produced extremely impoverished areas of cities, within which some social movements would take root; squatters movements were an archetypal form of protest. Though somewhat anomalous in other ways, the South African rent strike that began in September 1984 is one example. Here rent strikes were sparked by rent rises on government-owned homes in black townships of 25–88 per cent in the early 1980s. Though aiming at rent control and rent reduction these strikes also developed broader political aims, such as the recognition of traditional leadership at a local level, that challenged some institutions of apartheid. By 1988, 90 per cent of tenants had joined the strikes, developing a 'culture of nonpayment' that led to conflict with the post-apartheid African National Congress government of Nelson Mandela in 1997 (Corr 1999: 134–6). At the same time, other struggles emerged, often based or deriving strong support from universities. For example, students were prominent in the protests in Indonesia that led to the fall from power of President Abdurrahman Wahid. These protests focused on financial and political scandals associated with Wahid. They also continued a tradition of protest for political change that had faced severe repression under the long reign of President Suharto, had contributed to Suharto's fall and was not willing to ignore Wahid's perceived failure to reform authoritarian governance, reduce corruption and prosecute key Suharto beneficiaries. Such protests are often urban based, frequently leaning on strong youth and student support both for numbers in the street and the articulation of beliefs. The nature of these protests has shifted across different countries and different issues but the combination of urban, youth and student protest remained constant through the last quarter of the twentieth century. Such constancy is not clearly the case with the second strand of protest in the South.

The second area of protest in the South is insurrectionary protests, often conducted by armed guerrilla forces. This tradition of protest drew heart, tactics and ideas from such revolutionaries as Castro and Guevara in Cuba and Ho Chi Minh in Vietnam. The fundamental idea, often called Guevarism, was for a militant few to take to rural areas and from there build support for revolution through armed struggle (Guevara *et al.* 2002). Aiming at the seizure of state power, Che Guevara famously put these ideas into practice not only in Cuba but also in the Congo and Bolivia, where he met his death. Other guerrilla movements, not necessarily so closely allied to Marxist ideas as those that adopted Guevarism, have also emerged. Guerrillas in the Philippines have gained world attention by kidnapping and ransoming tourists, while guerrillas in Colombia have become the target of US anti-drug programmes and have helped create Colombia's internal warfare. These movements all focus on the state as a target that can be taken over through effective military tactics and grassroots organising. Such movements are often provoked by the desperate poverty of many Southern nations and the belief, not always misguided, that elites in these nations are serving the interests of the more powerful Northern nations while corruptly filling their own pockets. The exception to this model of guerrilla warfare are the Zapatistas of Mexico. The Zapatistas have transformed what guerrilla insurgency means, almost from a military to a social movement (Harvey 1998; Holloway and Pelaez 1998; Ross 2000). However, the effects of this on other guerrilla insurgencies, such as the Tamil Tigers, is at the time of writing wholly unclear.

Struggles over land and culture are the third key component of popular activism in the South. These involve two different types of communities, though they are also closely related: peasants and indigenous peoples. Sometimes this distinction is impossible to determine, but it is important to note as not all peasants are indigenous peoples and there may be conflicts between non-indigenous peasants and indigenous peasants, despite their common 'objective' interests. The struggle over land in Tacamiche Honduras demonstrates this type of struggle.

The company Chiquita Brands International ran a banana plantation in Tacamiche, employing mostly local people. In response to Chiquita's refusal to raise wages, in the context of Honduras's 30 per cent inflation rate, a strike was called. In 1994, Chiquita closed the plantation, despite Honduran law stating it was illegal to close a plantation in response to a strike. The local people, faced with no jobs, food or possibility of income in their local area, then took over part of the plantation, planting crops. Attempts at eviction were first defeated and then, in 1996, a surprise onslaught saw the local community lose virtually everything, as homes, crops, health centre and three churches were bulldozed. The local people refused to move into newly built relocated housing and organised a campaign that led to a partial victory in 1997. Government funds were provided to develop self-help industries and Chiquita rebuilt some of the houses and churches it had demolished (Corr 1999: 39–50).

Similar struggles can be seen across the South, with starvation wages or lack of jobs making the right to land often essential to survival for rural peoples. Indigenous peoples are often caught in this economic position and accompany this with cultural and spiritual ties to land. As the Australian Aborigines, in the developed world, say of themselves, 'the land does not belong to us, we belong to the land'. This has led to land rights claims and struggles that parallel peasant struggles but are overlaid with centuries of colonial repression, with nationally significant symbolic moments and attitudes to land and community that are in deep contradiction to the Northern or developed world's championing of monetarist economic systems.

All three types of struggle continued through the last quarter of the twentieth century, indeed had been going on for some time, with indigenous people's struggles reaching back to colonisations often over five hundred years old. What marks political struggle in all three of these types of activism in the South is a growing engagement with the global programme of monetarist or neo-liberal economic reform at the end of the twentieth century. Such programmes appeared to many as a new form of economic colonialism, and the three components of struggle increasingly engaged with the effects in their lands of changes being pushed onto their nations. Changes such as smaller states, greater freedom for capital, reduced rights for workers and increased deference to private (over communal) property rights.

We have outlined popular struggle in the South or developing world, and now will consider a final component of late twentieth-century activism: the radical right. Once this is introduced we will be in a position to look more closely at the anti-globalisation movement itself. The same political contexts set by revisions at national and international level of the state and its roles following the 1960s have seen the rise of new reactionary movements. These are distinct from the movements that have been followed so far but can also be connected to them. The difficulty posed by them is partially definitional, because with the demise of the left/right distinction it remains as problematic to describe new reactionary movements as 'inheritors of the right' as it is to describe the movements covered so far as 'inheritors of the left'. Difficulties arise here not least because left/right remains a powerful political axis, although as one among many rather than being the dominant one. In the space we have here we can note that there have been some inheritors of the right, even if that term is partially misleading, and that these have emerged alongside the social movements most relevant to hacktivism (Jordan 2002).

Some of these movements are close to or explicitly neo-fascist. The rise of the National Front in France or of the less successful British National Party in the United Kingdom reflects such politics, or at least an attempt to reinvent such politics. Similarly the rise of the Northern League in Italy reflected some elements of neo-fascism while allying them to a regional perspective (Della Porta and Diani 1999). At the same time a number of fundamentalist religious groups were (re-) emerging. Since September 11, there has been widespread coverage of Islamic fundamentalist groups. These also reflect shifts in geo-politics; Russia supported US attacks on Afghanistan whereas during the Cold War the United States had supported against Russian invasion those it attacked in 2001. In the United States itself, there has been a seeming rise in Christian fundamentalist groups that are associated with a militant opposition usually known as the Patriot movement (Castells 1997; Jordan 2002). In all these spiritually based fundamentalisms there is a reaction, based on authoritarian and anti-modern principles, to changes in the world. While these movements do not directly form the political context for hacktivists, it is useful to note them as part of social movement politics in the twenty-first century.

Having laid out the three main components of social movement history at the end of the twenty-first century with the North, South and reactionary movements, we can turn to the emergence of the anti-globalisation movement. This comes directly from some of the trends we have examined and can be seen best by introducing first the Zapatistas and then the J18 international day of protest. Then in the final section of this chapter we will examine what the anti-globalisation movement means and how it forms a context for hacktivism.

The anti-globalisation movement

On 1 January 1994 two events marked Mexico's future. First, the North American Free Trade Agreement (NAFTA) came into effect. This created an economic zone between Canada, the United States and Mexico. Second, a guerrilla army appeared in Mexico's southernmost state, taking over several towns and calling themselves the Zapatistas. These guerrillas were protesting against the ongoing colonial repression of Mexico's indigenous peoples, the removal of the right to land redistribution to peasants previously enshrined in the Mexican Constitution and, more generally, the expected effects of a neo-liberal economic regime demanded by NAFTA. After a short series of battles, the Zapatistas retreated in the face of the Mexican Army into the Lacandon Jungle to begin a social and political struggle that continues to this day (Collier 1998; Harvey 1998; Ross 2000; Weinberg 2000).

This struggle has gone through various stages while advancing a number of key demands. First, the Zapatistas have demanded the right of those working the land to collectively own land. Second, they have asserted the right of indigenous peoples to be considered fully part of the Mexican nation. Third, they opposed monetarist/neo-liberal programmes of economic change. All these demands come together into a call for a new democratic settlement that both includes indigenous peoples, taking account of their unique circumstances, and creates a new civil society for all Mexicans. This latter demand extended internationally, leading to a series of *Encuentro* (encounters) which attempted to form a global movement for a global civil society. Following the retreat of the Zapatistas into the mountains, their struggle has largely been symbolic, though danger, violence and the Mexican military dog their communities. In their spokesman Subcomandante Marcos, officially the leader of the Zapatista National Liberation Army (EZLN) but subordinate to the comandantes who lead the whole Zapatista struggle, they have a charismatic writer who has captured many imaginations (Marcos 2000). The Zapatistas have waged a powerful struggle of words, using appeals and arguments to form debates and create support. This has been greatly aided by support networks, particularly those that have helped form the strong Zapatista presence on the Internet. Finally, the Zapatistas have taken up internal struggles to form their own inclusive civil society, particularly by promulgating a 'woman's law' that significantly altered the place of women in indigenous communities and opens the struggle to wider issues than ones of land and rights (Rovira 2000).

By 2001 the Zapatistas, and supportive communities, had suffered massacres, been driven from established camps deeper into the jungle, been invaded time and again by Mexican troops and, more generally, seen their political resolve thoroughly tested. They had also created a national, grassroots-run plebiscite that endorsed many of their demands, entered negotiations with the Mexican government and generated worldwide support. In early 2001, the Zapatistas descended from the mountains and jungles, taking a bus tour around Mexico. Here they made links, gave speeches and called for social change. Finally, they arrived in Mexico City, addressing a huge outdoor rally and, eventually, being given the right to address the Mexican legislature. An insurrectionary community, with a guerrilla army, had freely travelled the nation and then addressed its representative government. Following this and the loss of the Mexican Presidency by the PRI (Revolutionary Institutional Party), which had held power for many years, it appeared that at least some of the new laws demanded by the Zapatistas were to be enacted. However, the new laws fell short of those demanded and were then reduced by the legislature to something unacceptable to the Zapatistas. The Zapatistas remain in the mountains and jungles, building autonomous communities, inspiring dissent and seeking social change. As we will see they form a key part both of the anti-globalisation movement and in the emergence of hacktivism.

On 18 June 1999 (J18), a global carnival against capital was held. Planned for months ahead, it involved demonstrations around the world, all aimed at capitalism and particularly at finance capitalists who were closely associated with international neo-liberal reforms. The demonstration in London involved four gigantic puppet heads each of which played music. Masks were handed out in four colours, that matched colours associated with each head, and on which were printed both reasons for the demonstration and a quote from an unnamed guerrilla (who was in fact Subcomandante Marcos). The playing of the theme from *Mission Impossible* signalled those with each coloured mask to follow their head. Eluding and confusing police, they met up again in front of the London International Financial Futures and Options Exchange (LIFFE) which was literally walled in behind a quickly built brick wall. This symbolised the rejection of finance capital by focusing on a futures exchange, where trades essentially bet on the future prices of commodities. Violence marked this demonstration, including the trashing of a McDonald's. Other, sometimes less elaborate, protests were held worldwide. In Melbourne, the leader of the Federal opposition was hit by a custard cream pie while he spoke about global trade. In Nigeria, thousands welcomed the return of Ken Saro-Wiwa's son with a carnival of the oppressed (Saro-Wiwa was executed by the Nigerian government). And there were other actions around the world (see http://bak.spc.org/j18/site/). The global nature of the protest and its clear focus on a certain economic system as its target marked one of the key points when a movement became a global movement with a common enemy.

Later in 1999, the now famous protest against the World Trade Organisation meeting in Seattle marked the explosion of the anti-globalisation movement into wide, public consciousness. Clearly linked to an international struggle against neo-liberal forms of globalisation, J18 and Seattle provided a model of demonstration, in particular for Northern activists, which was to be followed in subsequent years (Starr 2000). This consisted of attempting to block the meeting of the international institutions promoting neo-liberal programmes of globalisation. Along this model demonstrations attempted to disrupt, and sometimes succeeded, the IMF and World Bank meeting in Prague, the Quebec summit seeking to extend a NAFTA-like agreement throughout Central and Southern America, the G8 meeting in Genoa and more. At the same time, struggles such as those already outlined as broadly typical of Southern protests continued and increasingly became linked to anti-globalisation protests. Meetings such as the FSM (Forum Social Mundial/World Social Forum) in Porto Alegre, Brazil, link together protests, both across and within Southern and Northern areas.

All these protests and actions have led to the naming of the movement as the anti-globalisation movement, though this is clearly misleading as the movement is based on opposition to a certain form of globalisation. Like all social movements it has diverse, sometimes contradictory, elements and ideas but it also campaigns along a broad front against the international programme of neo-liberal reform. While no one organisation or set of ideas captures the nature of the anti-globalisation movement, we can conclude this tracing of its emergence by touching on the People's Global Action (PGA) organisation. This was formed in 1998 by activists protesting in Geneva against the second Ministerial Conference of the WTO, and to celebrate the fiftieth anniversary of the multilateral trade system (GATT and WTO). PGA is an attempt to create a worldwide alliance against neo-liberal globalisation and it defined five hallmarks for participating in this alliance, which are perhaps the best way of summarising the anti-globalisation movement's aims (www.agp.org).

1   A very clear rejection of the WTO and other trade liberalisation agreements (such as APEC, the EU, NAFTA, etc.) as active promoters of a socially and environmentally destructive globalisation.

2   We reject all forms and systems of domination and discrimination including, but not limited to, patriarchy, racism and religious fundamentalism of all creeds. We embrace the full dignity of all human beings.

3   A confrontational attitude, since we do not think that lobbying can have a major impact in such biased and undemocratic organisations, in which transnational capital is the only real policymaker.

4   A call to non-violent civil disobedience and the construction of local alternatives by local people, as answers to the action of governments and corporations.

5   An organisational philosophy based on decentralisation and autonomy.

The most recent significant development in the anti-globalisation movement has seen the strains of globalisation helping to destabilise some nation-states. This has been particularly pronounced through Latin America in the early twenty-first century. The most developed example is Argentina, where an economic collapse has led to the proliferation of local democracies which work around or ignore institutionalised government, a wave of factory takeovers with subsequent production being developed under some local worker control and a series of protests uniting across social divisions of all sorts. Artist-activist John Jordan summarised Argentina this way:

> Observing an entire society creatively dealing with complete economic collapse in Argentina. Hearing about the government being deposed by the sound of millions of clashing pots and pans. Watching bankrupt factories being occupied and run by the employees themselves, witnessing those who have nothing experimenting with ways to grow food and work autonomously from capitalist systems, listening to neighbourhood assemblies debate the future of their communities, practising direct democracy without leaders or representative, while standing in a circle on a Buenos Aires street corner.
>
> (Jordan 2003)

Activists have been arguing that the changes in Argentina are deeply significant, because they add to the array of anti-globlisation protests the potential that protest may lead to the reconstruction of a whole nation-state. The spectre of popular revolution, first reasserted symbolically by the Zapatistas, has re-emerged as a potential reality. Of course, nothing is certain about the future of Argentina, or the anti-globalisation movement, but instead of arguing how a new world 'might' come into being, Argentina might show the being of a new world.

What is the anti-global movement?

This anti-globalisation movement took shape simultaneously with the emergence of hacktivism and forms its key political context. To conclude this scene setting, it is appropriate to ask: What is the anti-globalisation movement? Movements with a global focus are not new, whether we think of the past thirty years, for example in the modern green movement, or the past two hundred, for example in the anti-slavery movement. Yet, in the last five, at most ten, years of the twentieth century, something called the 'anti-globalisation movement' emerged. What meaning can we give to this phrase? What is it that has formed the central, most important political context for hacktivism?

For a start we know the term 'anti-globalisation' is a misnomer. The movement is not anti some forms of globalisation and drawing on Chapter 2 we can see the movement might have been called 'viral protest' or 'anti-viral society'. The problem when trying to define social and political movements is that these movements are not simply unified or straightforwardly coherent. Rather they are agglomerations of organisations, ideas, events, actions, publications, struggles and individuals. Contradictions and complexities make up social movements, not the unity of a political party's organisation and manifesto. To grasp the anti-globalisation movement can only mean passing over some of the meanings of globalisation and the viral society the movement is engaged with. This will not define the movement by its opposition or pull all possible meanings and actions together into one coherent package. Rather, it will indicate the breadth, complexity and uncertainty of the anti-globalisation movement. What then is the 'globalisation' that the anti-globlisation movement fights: an ideology; an economic programme; a new imperialism; a cultural agenda; a technology; a remembrance?

An ideology   Or more specifically neo-liberalism as the ideology or virus of a particular type of globalisation. This is a set of ideas also known as Reaganomics/Thatcherism which hold individual freedom as their core principle or 'good', against the evil of collective, especially governmental/state ventures. At its heart this ideology wishes to destroy community, association, mutuality and collectivity worldwide in the search for a system that rewards the individual for competing in the 'correct' fashion. But how do you compete correctly?

An economic programme   This is, in many ways, an attempt to enact the neo-liberal ideology just outlined; in other views it is simply the latest stage of capitalism. It is a set of economic precepts for 'opening' up global trade in a free market context, pursued and enacted by international bodies such as the WTO with the fundamental backing of the United States. It has familiar aims such as reducing government, freeing up entrepreneurs, trickling down wealth, crippling welfare; we are all familiar, perhaps too familiar, with its slogans and tenets. It defines how you compete correctly in globalised capitalism. It defines the free market as one free for corporations but unfree for unions, communities or movements in struggle against the consequences of this particular free market.

A new imperialism Not just a set of ideas or an economic system, we also see around us a new chapter in the inglorious, exploitative and vicious history of imperialism. It is a post-colonial domination in which there is only one power capable of imposing its will worldwide, the United States, around which gather most of the overdeveloped nations which proliferate and celebrate its viral politics. It is an economic form, closely allied to the globalisation economic programme, in which value is extracted from developing or poorer nations – particularly through militarised 'economic zones' – on the 'promise' of gaining the bottom rung of industrialisation's long, bitter ladder. It is also a globalised security form, dependent on terrorist threats and a heightened sense of fear and danger among the wealthy for its impetus, and reliant on the big sticks carried by the United States and its friends.

A cultural agenda The oft-noted homogenisation of world culture goes hand in hand with a fragmentation and differentiation of means of producing and exchanging symbols and signs. It is not just the creation of ever-larger media corporations but also the grassroots' ability to self-produce symbols and meanings, such as in fanzines or the Internet. It is not just the wearing of Gap world-over, the ubiquity of the golden arches and the swoosh but also hideaway places where other cultures are remembered and reinvigorated. It is the ability of the Internet to put the supporters of the Zapatista and Patriot movements in the public domain. It is the dominance of Hollywood-produced films as well as a golden age of Bollywood-produced films and grassroots productions, such as those of Big Noise, which filmed, cut and edited a documentary on the Zapatista caravan that was shown the day after the Zapatistas arrived in Mexico City.

A technology Specifically, information and communication technologies most powerfully symbolised by the Internet. Technologies that allow global transmission of information that both enables the ever-more powerful, ever-faster international financial markets and underpins global dissemination of information to support and create protest.

A remembrance   Almost against itself, within globalisation has arisen the unmistakeable reminders of times before; a remembrance most obviously and powerfully represented in indigenous people's resistances. From the seminal revolt in the Chiapas to the worrying essentialism of Fijian extremists, indigenous peoples have refused to be lost, have refused to do nothing more than just 'not die'. In a time of accelerated globalisation, in which nations exchange people, symbols, money, guns and laws at ever-increasing rates, we have communities of today with roots deep in a 'deep' past.

As part of and against these senses of the word 'globalisation' we have also *a new form of protest*. It is in protest that globalisation's true contours begin to be perceived: it is only with the Zapatistas that the meaning of a North American Free Trade Association becomes clear; it is only with hacktivism that the politics of the Internet is uncovered; it is only with culture jamming that the absurdities of postmodern advertising are laid bare; it is only with McSpotlight and McLibel that the breadth, depth and unsavoury nature of McCultures are detailed; and so on (Jordan 2002). In resistance comes revelation and here we circle from globalisation to grasp the importance of change; anti, globalisation and movement are the three terms that name one project for global change. Depending on our timescale we can locate the recent movement as, perhaps, a shift from the DiY cultures that included (at least) eco-activist, animal liberation and pleasure-seeking raving politics of the 1990s; or as, perhaps, the latest development in a series of social movements born in late 1960s and that continue to this day; or as, perhaps, another moment in the series of popular struggles throughout the twentieth century reaching back at least as far as the birth of anti-capitalism and beyond. This movement reaches back to re-teach the fundamental truth that the birth of liberation struggles comes with the birth of oppression.

The movement involves the famous, such as Subcomandante Insurgente Marcos, and the everyday, such as individual decisions to boycott sweatshop-produced goods. It takes in symbolic actions, such as those run by Adbusters, and can be as embodied an action as you can get, such as riots and guerrilla warfare. The movement stretches, perhaps more symbolically than actually, from the revolt of the Chiapas through the realisation that a broad movement had developed with events such as J18 and Seattle and into the futures.

The end and beginning of the millennium

The events of September 11 placed a question mark over the anti-globalisation movement. There has been a crack down on political dissent in the overdeveloped nations that feel themselves suddenly besieged by terror; detention without trial, the use of military courts, the redefinition of dissent as terrorism. Movements and actions in the developing or underdeveloped world face even greater repression; whereas activists face legal repression in the overdeveloped world elsewhere they face violent repression. With the development of the 'war on terrorism' into a war of barely concealed imperial control against Iraq, it might be thought the space of protest had dramatically narrowed.

Yet, as already noted, social eruptions in Argentina continued to add the possibility of social revolution to the dreams of anti-globalisation. Protests against the war on Iraq itself pushed many millions onto the streets, leading who now knows where when people begin to reflect on their sudden mobilisation. The spaces of protest continue in a more militarised, more aggressive environment, but nothing shows them disappearing or even diminishing.

Viewing these changes it is impossible for us to know the future but it is equally impossible to ignore the past. The trends this chapter has identified toward the coexistence of a multiplicity of social movements within popular protest and, as we will see in this book, the integration of hacktivism within these protests can be observed stretching back nearly forty years. These trends will not suddenly disappear, equally they will not continue unaffected. Possible inflections can be guessed at. The Western or Northern anti-globalisation movement, which was already undergoing a searching self-examination before September 11, prompted by the protests at Genoa in the summer of 2001, may dissipate as individual struggles return to closer, often more local, concerns. The powerful integrative forces driving the emergence of the anti-globalisation movement may be destroyed through the repression of the state and the uncertainty of those in the movement itself. Or the integrative forces may be too strong, they may reflect needs and struggles that are too deeply felt for them to dissipate so soon after becoming articulated. Or (perhaps most likely?), somewhere in-between its failure or its global mobilisation, the anti-globalisation movement, North and South, will continue to contest some of the central conflicts of twenty-first-century societies. In Chapter 4 we will examine hacktivism as a part of this struggle and these conflicts.

4 Mass action hacktivism

Anti-globalisation and the importance of bad technology

> The rules of cultural and political resistance have dramatically changed. The revolution in technology brought about by the rapid development of computers and video has created a new geography of power relations in the first world that could only be imagined as little as twenty years ago: people are reduced to data, surveillance occurs on a global scale, minds are melded to screenal reality, and an authoritarian power emerges that thrives on absence. The new geography is a virtual geography, and the core of political and cultural resistance must assert itself in this electronic space.
>
> (CAE 1994: 3)

Hacktivism

The previous chapters have set the scene in terms of the various generations of the hacking community, the viral state of society and the evolution of the protest community. First, we saw how the hacking community had developed from a pioneering and, almost, innocent exploration of technology into a multifaceted community encompassing a wide range of technological interventions, all of which somehow touch on the 'hack'. Then we explored the nature of a society increasingly interpretable as a body permeated by the spreading of virus-like immaterial commodities and computer and biological viruses. Finally, we brought ourselves as up to date as possible with popular protest, particularly noting the nature of the anti-globalisation movement. In the mid-1990s, all three of these influences crossed over and one result was hacktivism: online direct action. Now we can set out the two key trends within hacktivism, and in doing so we shall see repeatedly the varying influences of the three interlocking contexts of hacking, protest and viral informational societies.

This chapter explores mass action hacktivism. This is the kind of online action most closely associated with the anti-globalisation movement. Here we find the most direct attempts to turn 'traditional' forms of radical protest, such as street demonstrations, into forms of cyberspatial protest. Chapter 5 will explore what can be called 'digitally correct' hacktivism, that is online direct actions that are influenced perhaps more by the history and technical concerns of hacking than by the more direct political concerns of anti-globalisation protests. However, in both cases this is a matter of emphasis rather than exclusion. Mass action hacktivism and digitally correct hacktivism are both formed in the context of hacking, protest and viral times, but each draws more influence from some of these contexts than others.

A further term needs a quick introduction now that we are dealing directly with hacktivism and hacktivist actions: *direct action*. This is more often attached to non-violence in the term non-violent direct action (nvda), which covers a range of protests such as sit-ins, boycotts and so on. However, for two reasons it is direct action more than non-violence that concerns hacktivism. First, one of us has argued that the development of social movements in the twenty-first century has led to direct action gaining in importance over non-violence (Jordan 2002: 60–9). Second, the notion of violence in cyberspace involves complexities, if not at times absurdities, because the conception of non-violence prevalent in social movements involves an inherent physicality that is absent in cyberspace (Jordan 2002: 119–35). For these reasons it is more important to focus on direct action in relation to hacktivism than to explore nvda as a whole.

Direct action means what it says: it is the attempt to effect political change immediately. It does not involve one tactic but a whole range of different possibilities including:

> *boycotts* attempt to effect change by starving out opponents
> *blockades* attempt to halt movements to and from disputed places
> *strikes* stop work in order to gain changes
> *civil disobedience* ignores unjust laws.

Direct action involves taking some kind of stand, in order to effect a change as immediately as possible. It is sometimes not possible to alter directly a disputed political object, for example laws can be ignored or transgressed (mass trespassing for instance) but for the final change to be won there has to be a secondary moment when legal change is effected. Direct action is not only the behaviour of activists 'in the field' but is also the effects that are supposed to flow from these actions.

Hacktivism attempts to translate the principles of direct action into virtuality. The sit-in or blockade that occurs in the streets and aims to cause a meeting to fail, can be matched by a blockade of online messages, which aims to make computer support for the meeting fail. We will find in what follows an exploration of two types of this direct action: mass action hacktivism and digitally correct hacktivism.

Mass action hacktivism is a combination of politics and inefficient technology. It is an attempt to defy the lack of physicality in online life, in favour of a mass collection of virtual bodies that are yet not present to each other. Mass action hacktivism is the closest to traditional mass protest that has been seen on the Internet.

Digitally correct hacktivism is the political application of hacking to the infrastructure of cyberspace. It is an attempt to use the lack of physicality in online life to amplify a political message. Digitally correct hacktivism flows within the structures of online life, using its powers and will be detailed in Chapter 5.

The first calls for turning offline protest into online protest argued it was key to build on the Internet's peculiar forms of power, yet when the first actions inspired by such calls were developed they had transformed themselves into actions that contradicted the Internet's powers. To see this and fully introduce mass action hacktivism, we can look at the Critical Arts Ensemble's calls for electronic civil disobedience, beginning in 1994, and then at one of the earliest hacktivist actions, the Electronic Disturbance Theatre's support of the Zapatistas. Following this we shall look in more detail at a case study of mass action hacktivism and then at the connections between mass action hacktivism, the anti-globalisation movement and what is called culture jamming. Finally, we will conclude by delineating mass action hacktivism's self-contradictory, yet potentially effective, structures.

Theory and practice: Critical Arts Ensemble and the Electronic Disturbance Theatre

The year 1994 marks a dividing line in the Internet's history; it was the year the World Wide Web began to make its impact, having been invented only in 1993. It is also the year that the Critical Arts Ensemble

(CAE) articulated a dividing line in political activism. They claimed that 'power' had transferred itself from static points, that can be targeted, to a nomadic existence in virtuality. Nomadism here meant being able to shift the locus of power constantly to avoid attacks. For example, a company may make T-shirts and use a tax-free zone in a developing country to do so. It is possible the workers in that zone may try to become organised and effect some change in the rules for the tax-free zone. The response in days of flexible production systems can often be simply to move the production to somewhere else which offers better terms. Here the locus of power, a factory as a place in which relations of oppression can be contested, is simply moved to avoid a confrontation and re-establish relations of dominance. Such a move relies on virtuality in many senses, perhaps particularly for the ability to pass designs and specifications to factories and to find and organise new factory spaces. However, the key nomadic power here is money which, flowing through global financial systems, is able to shift rapidly from one nation or trade area to another, underpinning the use of physical assets like factories. This example intermingles virtual and non-virtual nomadism to demonstrate CAE's point: 'Elite power, having rid itself of its national and urban bases to wander in absence on the electronic pathways, can no longer be disrupted by strategies predicated upon the contestation of sedentary forces' (CAE 1994: 23).

CAE argue that this poses a problem for resistance and protest, which have been implicitly reliant on the physicality of protest. It appears no longer to matter if unions in a certain factory become organised because production simply can be shifted to a place with a more compliant workforce. Similarly, the significance of thousands protesting in the streets may be seriously diminished if finance can flee that country for more ruthlessly controlled societies. And if it no longer matters if this road here is blocked or that supermarket site is camped upon, because place is no longer relevant and all blockages can be moved around, then many, if not most, protest tactics will be rendered ineffective. At least, this is the picture CAE painted in the mid-1990s of the future of resistance:

> CAE has said it before, and we will say it again: as far as power is concerned, the streets are dead capital! Nothing of value to the power elite can be found on the streets, nor does this class need control of the streets to efficiently run and maintain state institutions. For CD [civil disobedience] to have any meaningful effect,

the resisters must appropriate something of value to the state. Once they have an object of value, the resisters have a platform from which they may bargain for (or perhaps demand) change.

(CAE 1996: 11)

And objects of value reside in the networks now.

Electronic civil disobedience is the obvious and immediate answer for CAE; the translation of classic civil disobedience tactics into the virtual realm. Civil disobedience consists of a range of tactics, all of which retract the normal life of a society in order to disrupt those who are targeted by the protest. People may sit in front of machines tearing up a woodland, using their bodies to prevent the woodland disappearing. People might refuse to pay taxes as a way of disputing their validity. In the terms CAE use to understand civil disobedience, it is a way of forming blockages in systems of dominance. Classic civil disobedience tends to find embodied ways of creating blockages, whether it is the body put into the danger of a sit-down protest or the body tramping the streets in a mass demonstration.

CAE's revision of civil disobedience retains the notion of blockage, which fits perfectly with their conception of dominant powers having become flows of information, but reconceives what blockage means. They argue that having shifted from essentially physically based realms, blockage must become a stopper in information flow. These blockages turn out not to need mass action anymore but can be created on the basis of expertise developed by hackers. CAE see hackers in league with activists, allowing the targeting of the destructive weapons of cyberspace on political targets: 'Nomadic power must be resisted in cyberspace rather than in physical space. . . . A small but co-ordinated group of hackers could introduce electronic viruses, worms, and bombs into the data banks and programmes, and networks of authority' (CAE 1994: 25). CAE believe that the expertise hackers develop in the technologies of cyberspace can offset the imbalance of power that activists are seeking to redress. Electronic civil disobedience magnifies its effects not by increasing the numbers of bodies involved in protest, as happens in civil disobedience, but by using the expertise of hackers to increase their political effects. The changed nature of cyberspace offers an opportunity for those campaigning against dominant powers to equalise the political game, and for CAE the equaliser is a politicised hacker community.

Unfortunately, this politicisation was not one CAE believed existed, 'No alliance exists between hackers and specific political organisations.

In spite of the fact that each would benefit through interaction and cooperation, the alienating structure of a complex division of labor keeps these two social segments separated more successfully than could the best police force' (CAE 1996: 19). However, within two years of their calls for electronic civil disobedience a one-time member of CAE, Ricardo Dominguez, was part of a group developing one of the first forms of electronic civil disobedience, which was direct political action, theory and artform all in one. It is was eventually called the *FloodNet* or the Swarm and was mounted in support of the Zapatistas by the Electronic Disturbance Theatre (EDT) (Meikle 2002: 140–72).

Electronic Disturbance Theatre was formed in 1998 by four artist-hacker-activists and it retained this multidimensional approach for FloodNet its earliest major project. This project further developed protests in support of the Zapatista struggle by connecting it to the early development of the anti-globalisation movement. These protests developed civil disobedience in cyberspace by targeting websites and online connections of various authorities which were seen to be supporting the repression of the Zapatista uprising. For example, key targets tended to be the Mexican President's online site and the Pentagon. Here is a short account of the first actions taken by EDT.

> In solidarity with the Zapatista movement we welcome all netsurfers with ideals of justice, freedom, solidarity and liberty within their hearts, to a virtual sit-in. On January 29, 1998 from 4:00 p.m. GMT (Greenwich Mean Time) to 5:00 p.m. (in the following five web sites, symbols of Mexican neoliberalism): Bolsa Mexicana de Valores: http://www.bmv.com.mx Grupo Financiero Bital: http://www.bital.com.mx Grupo Financiero Bancomer: http://www.bancomer.com.mx Banco de Mexico: http://www.banxico.org.mx Banamex: http://www.banamex.com
>
> Technical instructions: Connect with your browser to the upper mentioned web sites and push the button 'reload' several times for an hour (with in between an interval of few seconds).
>
> (Dominguez 1998)

Immediately we can see that the CAE conception of electronic civil disobedience has been inverted. Instead of a small cadre of highly trained activists and hackers interacting to create protest, we have here a low-level of technical knowledge (effectively the ability to run a browser on the World Wide Web) combined with a request for large numbers to participate. The idea is that if a lot of people load up the targeted websites and then all press reload many times, a large number of requests will be made to the targeted sites. If enough requests are made in a short enough time to a targeted site then it will become overloaded and either function slowly or collapse altogether.

This protest was called a virtual sit-in by EDT and it mirrored closely non-cyberspatial sit-ins. A body was required behind each connection to the targeted sites. The repeated reloading is the virtual equivalent of staying in the one place. The style of electronic disobedience is almost wilfully contrary to the nature of cyberspace, in its desire to overcome the disembodied nature of cyberspace and to recreate the effects of a protest of many people. In contrast, CAE had originally called for protests by small numbers of people whose powers were magnified by expertise. Soon after the virtual sit-in, protests more like those envisaged by CAE did occur.

> a group of Mexican digital activists on February 4, 1998 hacked into a Mexican government home page on the Internet and placed pro-Zapatista slogans on the front pages of the site. Soon afterwards an MS Dos Ping Action program from the ECD group arrived to hit Mexican Banks and Chase Manhattan Bank on February 9.
>
> (Dominguez 1998)

Here two actions undertaken by smaller groups, with no need for mass intervention, took place. One action was to hack the Mexican government website. Pictures of Emeliano Zapata appeared on the site, along with slogans such as 'We're watching you, big brother!' Such actions require only one person, though several could be involved, to crack the website and replace its pages. An MS-Dos Ping Action program is a piece of software that can generate numerous requests to a targeted site (pings being small requests sent to a site to return basic information). With large numbers of pings targeted at one site, this is an automated replication of the blocking technique used for the virtual sit-in. If enough pings are generated the targeted site will slow down or collapse entirely. Again this is an action that can be taken either by one person or by a small number of people in concert with each other.

In subsequent years, EDT developed the virtual sit-in form of protest in contrast to the more CAE-theorised forms and other groups joined in developing politically comparable protests. We shall examine in more detail some of these below. The point here is that at the birth of electronic civil disobedience there were two clear possibilities; one was conceived from the nature of cyberspace and one operated in contradiction to the nature of cyberspace. What is now clear is that mass action developed mainly the latter and not the former. The mass action, which gains legitimacy from involving mass numbers of people and not by the effects it generates, would come to dominate the strand of hacktivism most closely associated with the anti-globalisation movement, and other radical causes, at the end of the twentieth century.

This brief comparison of theory and practice at the beginning of mass action hacktivism will now be illustrated more clearly through a detailed case study, which will show how online direct action operated in contradiction to cyberspace's disembodied nature and not in concert with it.

Seattle and the World Trade Organisation

The protest against the World Trade Organisation in Seattle in late 1999 was a key event in the late twentieth century anti-globalisation movement. It was not, as it is sometimes thought to be, an isolated moment or the first moment of a new process. Rather, it was a culmination, a point at which a movement emerged clearly, both into public view and into the consciousness of activists. It happened for two reasons. First, the event was in the United States, and was the first of a series of anti-globalisation carnival-protests to occur there. Taking place in the United States gained this event worldwide attention in a way that perhaps had not occurred with similar protests, whether they happened in global cities like London or in wilderness areas such as the Lacandon Jungle. Second, all the elements of the anti-globalisation movement were present at Seattle, in a way that made it both a culmination and departure point for anti-globalisation struggles. And mass virtual direct action was there.

The virtual direct action that coincided with the Seattle street protests operated perfectly in tune with those protests. The aim on the streets of Seattle was to halt or disrupt the World Trade Organisation conference by preventing delegates from entering the conference venue. To that end traditional civil disobedience and direct actions were employed, blocking streets with bodies through mass demonstrations and so on. The online protest employed similar tactics. Its aim was to block the computer network servicing the WTO meeting by flooding it with requests. The action was run by a hacktivist group called the

Electrohippies (or ehippies), which by 2002 was semi-retired, but was active in hacktivist actions at the end of the 1990s and the early years of the twenty-first century. The ehippies claim the action was successful overall, with the WTO conference networks being constantly slowed, brought to a complete total halt on two occasions and with 450,000 people (or technically computers) participating over five days (Electrohippies Collective 2000).

In form the virtual and street protests were closely allied. Both sought to block flows to the conference; on the streets flows of people and supplies were blocked, on the Internet flows of packets carrying information were blocked. In both cases, the overall aim was to prevent the conference, in order to prevent the most visible global neo-liberal organising institution from functioning. There are many examples of mass, online direct actions but it is arguable that the Electrohippies' actions for Seattle 1999 are the most obvious and emblematic ever undertaken. It is accordingly worth examining the nature of this demonstration in more detail.

The ehippies ran what is now a familiar aspect of cyberspace: a denial-of-service (DOS) action. As we have seen with the EDT, this consists of bombarding a targeted computer with so many messages (in Internet terminology, these are called packets) in such a short space of time that the target ceases to function. A first key distinction is between *centralised* and *distributed* denial of service. The distinction here is between attacking packets that come from one source, so that A is attacking B, or packets coming from many sources, so that A, C, D, E, etc. are all attacking B. In the main, DOS attacks are distributed (DDOS) because it is too easy to block, trace and catch an attacker if they launch all their packets from one site. It is within distributed denial-of-service (DDOS) attacks that the Electrohippies distinguished their actions at Seattle from usual DDOS attacks, by drawing a distinction between *automated* and *client-side* attacks. To see this distinction, which uncovers the heart of mass virtual direct actions, we need to digress briefly and outline the more familiar server-side DDOS attack. There have been many such attacks, and well-resourced and known sites, such as online auction house eBay.com and merchant Amazon.com, have been taken offline almost immediately by a DDOS attack. One incident that is well documented was that in May 2001 against Internet security researcher Steve Gibson.

Gibson runs a website that he uses to post analyses and fixes for security problems he has identified on the Internet. For example, on his site you can test, for free, how visible your computer is to others over the Internet. You do this by asking his site to try to find your own on the Internet and it then reports to you what security holes there might be. Gibson has other similar tools available on his website, but the main point here is that though a small fish in the Internet sea, Gibson is an Internet expert. On 4 May 2001 Gibson's website simply dropped off the Internet; it disappeared from cyberspace. When he analysed what was going on it turned out his two fast (T-1) connections to the Internet were being flooded with packets which prevented any information being sent back out from his site. For one type of packet over a certain period the normal traffic of 12,248,097 suddenly leapt to 54,528,114. The website had drowned. Once the attack was analysed and he was able to contact engineers from his Internet Service Provider filters could be put in place and suddenly, Gibson's site reappeared (Gibson 2001).

Gibson worked out that 474 other computers attached to the Internet had attacked his website. This meant the hacker had infected 474 other computers so that they simultaneously launched programs that targeted Gibson's site. Each of these computers had hidden within it what is called an irc-bot or sometimes a zombie, these are programs that run the attacks. This is what is meant by distributed in this case, though designed and run by a single person this attack was distributed across many computers. Five or more additional attacks followed and they seemed to be ongoing. Gibson kept an eye out on various hacker forums and one day a note appeared from someone claiming to be running the attacks who called himself Wicked and claimed to be 13 years old; it later turned out two others were helping Wicked. After he managed to reach out to Wicked, through some other hackers, and convince him to stop, Gibson was subsequently subject to two further DDOS attacks, each using more advanced and changed technologies. One of Gibson's conclusions was that such attacks are almost impossible to defend against (Gibson 2001).

The attacks on Gibson represent the mainstream of DDOS, working through the centralised control of distributed zombies or bots. The attack is distributed but automated; each of the 474 bots that attacked Gibson could be ordered to begin by the one person. Although this was a DDOS, in terms of control it was a centralised attack. Through these methods individual hackers can attack the largest online enterprises with extremely good chances of success. Cyberspace's immateriality and its ability to magnify expertise-based powers leads in this case to an extremely powerful and difficult to stop means of blocking flows to particular cyber-places, all with a method that one person can utilise (Jordan 1999a).

The Electrohippies turned these conventions on their head to form what they see as an ethical use of DDOS. The methods used by those like Wicked can be described as automated and centralised. The Electrohippies developed what they called a client-side DDOS, whose central feature was that each client or end computer had to choose to initiate the attack on its own, thereby depending on many people to initiate a mass action.

> What *the electrohippies* did for the WTO action was a *client-side distributed DoS action*. The electrohippies method of operation is also truly distributed since instead of a few servers, there were tens of thousands of *individual computer users* involved in the action. The requests sent to the target servers are generated by ordinary Internet users using their own desktop computer and (usually) a slow dial-up link. That means client-side distributed actions require the efforts of real people, taking part in their thousands simultaneously, to make the action effective. If there are not enough people supporting then the action doesn't work. The fact that service on the WTO's servers was interrupted on the 30th November and the 1st of December, and significantly slowed on the 2nd and 3rd of December, demonstrated that there was significant support for the *electrohippies* action.
>
> (Electrohippies Collective 2000)

The Electrohippies implemented this by writing a program that identified the targeted WTO computer and sent repeated requests to it. To be run someone had to choose to go to an Electrohippies webpage, which explained that the WTO was being targeted and that clicking on the next link would download and begin the attacking program (a java applet). Only if an individual then took the step of clicking on the next link would one attack begin. Once someone initiated a click, that individual's computer downloaded the program and began to attack; information began to bombard the WTO network and to help to block it. The crucial distinction was that rather than one or a few people setting in train a mass of automated attacks, the Electrohippies method required a mass of people to set in train individualised attacks. The Electrohippies did not ignore the Internet's power to magnify individual actions but limited their use of it in the following way. The ehippies site offered two links that downloaded slightly different versions of their attack program, one link was for fast connections and one for slow. The program for fast connections constantly reloaded six targeted pages on the WTO network, while the program for slow connections constantly reloaded three targeted pages. The ehippies utilised, in a minor way, the immateriality of the Internet while at the same time establishing the mass nature of their protest.

A different way of grasping the technological inefficiency built into the Electrohippies' conception, as against Wicked's attack on Gibson, is to assess the expertise needed by anyone to participate in these different types of DDOS. To participate in the Electrohippies' action all that was required was access to an Internet browser, knowledge of how to click on a link within the browser and knowledge of how to find the ehippies site. This level of expertise is as minimal as cyberspace allows; connect to the World Wide Web, find a website and click on links. The difficulty of finding a website is similar to knowing about a demonstration, which given the search facilities of the Web is possibly easier to do in cyberspace than it is in non-virtual spaces. For the type of DDOS Wicked launched against Steve Gibson, a far higher level of technical expertise is needed: an understanding of DDOS, the ability to find and use zombies or 'bots', the ability to target and understand Internet Protocol (IP) addresses and so on. The type of attack Wicked and friends launched required much higher levels of technical expertise than the Electrohippies' DDOS. The point of this quick comparison is that both these attacks seek to do fundamentally the same thing – to slow or halt a targeted computer by bombarding it with too much information. However, the Electrohippies ignored the type of attack Wicked launched, even though they certainly knew about and most likely had the expertise to conduct such an attack. The Electrohippies ignored this form of attack for political reasons.

> What we're all about is bringing *community accountability* to the Internet. Governments and corporations are setting up stall on the 'Net in the expectation that the space is immune from the normal pressure present in society like a new frontier. . .. but it isn't. We have to treat cyberspace as if it were another part of society. Therefore, we must find mechanisms for lobbying and protest in cyberspace to complement those normally used in real life. Without public pressure cyberspace will have no moral or normative controls

to control the excesses of politicians, groups or corporations who would seek to dominate that public space.

(Electrohippies Collective 2000)

To bring popular protest to cyberspace is the key goal of mass virtual direct action. To do this requires subverting the technical efficiency of the Internet. To create one of the now best-known attacks, integrated into a key moment in the development of the anti-globalisation movement, the ehippies had to act against the nature of the Internet. The ehippies had to re-embody each attacking program, ensuring in some way that each program attacking the WTO networks could be, roughly, equated with a protestor. Instead of the technical efficiency of zombie programs, each acting under one command, the ehippies enabled a technically inefficient assertion of mass virtual action.

Direct action or symbolic protest?

Mass virtual direct actions (mvdas), we can now see, are like a combination of direct action and symbolic protest. Though often merged these two are different protest tactics. Direct actions attempt to effect some kind of change immediately, through the very taking of the action. Direct action at Seattle was to prevent a meeting taking place and whether the protest was publicised or not the direct action was still able to take place. Symbolic protests are attempts to register a disagreement with something. They are attempts to form moments which influence others to make social change. A peaceful demonstration is of this type, as it aims to bring many people on to the streets who demonstrate the legitimacy of the social change that is being requested. A petition is another example. The more signatures a petition obtains, the more legitimate it is hoped the demand becomes.

Mass online protests are a combination of these two types of actions, despite their main aim being to create direct actions. As often happens with analogies made between virtual and non-virtual spaces, meanings shift and the comparison can be seen to conceal as well as reveal.

As a symbolic demonstration mass action hacktivism seems odd, afterall, who sees the protest? The people who make the protest are all sat at different computers, potentially spread across the world. They cannot see each other and can only know how many others are protesting if the site that launches the protest implements some form of counter. The loss of physicality in cyberspace means a loss of so many parts of a demonstration: sights, sounds, smells and the elation or depression that can follow when it becomes clear just how many people have come together to protest. There are two groups who can tell how many have come together in any mvda, or at least can take some measure of it. Those who run the protest can check their records to see how many different computers connected and took up their call. Those who are targeted can check their records to see how many computers connected to them in the protest period. However, even this is hazy as it may not be clear at all from the records created whether a visitor to a site was a protestor or just someone who happened to visit during the protest time. The epic qualities of the best demonstrations, both in terms of size and drama, are lost in cyberspace. While mass action hacktivism can clearly be symbolic actions, and it can draw large numbers of people together to protest, some of the qualities of a symbolic demonstration are lost.

Demonstrations also have the ability to enrol people in a campaign, because they make people choose to alter their daily routines and to participate in a (mildly) transgressive act. In a similar way, people must both find out about and choose to participate in a mass online action. People must somehow make the decision to enrol themselves into such a protest. Online protests have the advantage of being able to pass on a great amount of information, in forms that mean people can take a little or explore a lot. In non-virtual spaces it is difficult to hand over more than a leaflet, even if volumes could be devoted to the particular cause. But in cyberspace volumes of information can be made available to anyone wanting to access it.

It has been pointed out that though this is true, it is perhaps an easy form of commitment that is being requested. The short and non-confrontational act of accessing a website and clicking on a link seems to many to involve both less time and a great deal less effort than going to a physical demonstration. As a member of digitally correct hacktivist group Cult of Dead Cow argued,

> I know from personal experience that there is a difference between street and on-line protest. I have been chased down the street by a baton-wielding police officer on horseback. Believe me, it takes a lot less courage to sit in front of a computer.
>
> (Ruffin 2000)

What distinguishes mass virtual direct actions from a symbolic demonstration, is the ability to demonstrate a large number of people have protested and the chance to enrol people into a particular struggle. Online mass action certainly is analogous to symbolic demonstrations in the non-virtual world, but it is also significantly different.

There are other limitations to the analogy between non-violent direct action and mass virtual direct action. In terms of being a direct action, a website or network is targeted and if the protest goes well it will be slowed or even stopped. Yet the target is different between real and virtual spaces and it may be that virtual targets can find easier ways to shift and move than non-virtual targets. A particular target in physical space can often be found and blocked because it cannot move. For example, there might be a company importing wood some protestors believe comes from endangered forests. This company can be blockaded by protestors standing in front of its gate; there will only be a certain number of entries and exits that trucks carrying wood can use, and it will be difficult for the wood to be relocated to a secret store. On the Internet, location is defined by a number called the IP address (Internet Protocol address). This number directs all who ask for it to the appropriate place in cyberspace. These numbers are held in a central database, which copies itself to a number of other databases, which are accessed by computers making up the Internet. In theory, for a virtual lumber yard to shift location all that is required is a change in number. In theory, it is easy to dodge an attack in cyberspace. Fortunately, for hacktivists, in practice administrative arrangements are needed to make the changes needed to dodge an attack, time is needed for the new number to propagate and, of course, once a new number is propagated it can then be updated by the demonstrators.

These are some of the limitations of mass action hacktivism or mass virtual direct action. These kinds of actions are marked by the desire to recreate civil disobedience in virtual realms and then by the effects of such a translation. Cyberspace does not operate to the same social and cultural rules as non-cyberspace, and making civil disobedience work in cyberspace has meant reaching a compromise between the physical embodiment of civil disobedience and the lack of physicality of the Internet (Jordan 1999a). The central result is the use of technologies that are inefficient in cyberspatial terms but are efficient in political terms. The central fact is that attacks like the WTO protest or the EDT's Zapatista support actions could have been run like Wicked's assault on Gibson, but they were not, both for political reasons and against the nature of cyberspace. We shall discuss this combination further below, but it is this particular assertion of politics within and against the technologies of virtuality that marks mass action hacktivism. Before turning to this conclusion, we shall consider how the anti-globalisation movement has been the source and most powerful context for mass action hacktivism by looking at how some related online protests integrate mass actions in the context of anti-globalisation.

Mass action hacktivism and culture jamming

> You reach down to pull your golf ball out of the hole and there, at the bottom of the cup is an ad for a brokerage firm. You fill your car with gas, there's an ad on the nozzle. You wait for your bank machine to spit out money and an ad pushing GICs scrolls by in the little window. You drive through the heartland and the view of the wheatfields is broken at intervals by enormous billboards. Your kids watch Pepsi and Snickers ads in the classroom.
>
> (Lasn 1999: 19)

> One two-dollar can of spray can reverse a hundred-thousand-dollar media campaign.
>
> (Rushkoff 1994: 281)

Electronic protest and direct action extends into areas of satirical performance. Here hacktivism meets what is more broadly called culture jamming. In exploring this conjunction we can see how closely mass action hacktivism is associated with the anti-globalisation movement.

Culture jamming combines the manipulation of semiotic codes with physical changes to capitalist products. Lasn describes the saturation of the cultural realm with corporate images as a form of ubiquitous mental pollution (Lasn 1999). Culture jamming engages directly with media noise and combines both the previous aspects of direct action and satire. Groups such as Adbusters use techniques such as 'billboard banditry' to make small but crucial changes to corporate adverts that create a process of 'subvertising'. After the *Exxon Valdez* disaster, for example, the San Francisco-based Billboard Liberation Front subverted a radio promotion poster so that instead of 'Hits Happen. New X-100' it read 'Shit Happens – New Exxon'. Broadly defined, the concept of culture jamming parallels the broad original interpretation of hacking as a mindset applicable to a heterogeneous range of artefacts. Culture jamming turns the original purpose of a cultural artefact or piece of communication back on itself to create the opposite outcome: a semiotic version of ju-jitsu.

This ju-jitsu does not always work. In fact it suffers from an inherent recuperability. Once culture jammers enter the empire of signs and begin their work re-manipulating the semiotic viruses transmitted by corporations, they risk being trapped there. Culture jammers can have their signs turned back against them, have their techniques appropriated by the very corporate entities they are attacking, and then find them being used to create new consumptive bugs. Culture jamming operates constantly within this tension between the 'hack' of a corporate virus which disturbs people's views of the world and having their message interpreted as just another moment in the viral production of consumption, for instance, when a clothes shop used Zapatista slogans, images and messages to sell its line of 'urbanwear' (Jordan 2002).

It has been suggested that Marx himself provided an early precedent for such a strategy when he and Engels: 'planned to penetrate the international wire agencies in Brussels, through a leftist press agency, in order to distribute their messages more widely' (Dyer-Witheford 1999: 42). Information technologies may be instrumental in extending the decontextualised abstract global reach of viral societies, but they also bring a degree of autonomy and empowerment to those who would seek to resist such a process. The networks that are used for commercial communications and surveillance can be reappropriated to reinforce grass-roots opposition; networks circulate struggle as well as commodities. In these gaps, culture jammers take up semiotic struggle.

The etoy campaign

The etoy campaign of 1999 is perhaps the highest point of cross over between hacktivism and culture jamming and is a useful example. In the late 1990s, during the boom time of Internet commerce, the online toy-sellers located at www.etoys.com realised that there was a site at www.etoy.com. The latter site had been established for many years, been longer on the Internet than etoys, and was devoted to subversive artistic interventions. The toy-selling etoys decided this was an unacceptable threat to their commercial prospects and took steps to close down etoy. First they offered to buy etoy and when, for artistic reasons, this was refused, they took steps to have their perceived rival closed down. On 29 November the toy-sellers obtained an injunction closing down the artists; coincidentally the share price of the toy-sellers was at a high point of US$67 per share around that time. From here battle was joined, with a wide array of online and offline activists becoming involved.

Offline a legal challenge was mounted to the toy-seller's assault. Online a number of initiatives were developed. There was a mass virtual direct action lasting two weeks against the perceived corporate aggression. This utilised some of EDT's FloodNet software and was vigorously fought by the toy-sellers technical staff. Symbolic actions also proliferated, including setting up mirroring web sites which parodied the toy-sellers while puncturing their corporate myth-making and making the protest plain in investor chat rooms and bulletin boards. There was a mass mailing of the toy-seller's staff informing them of their bosses' actions. Finally, there was the toy war platform, which sadly only became operational as the war had virtually been won. The platform was effectively a chat room with graphics, which cleverly used lego-like images of soldiers, and was meant to be a place in which actions could be co-ordinated (Grether 2000; Wishart and Boschler 2002).

In what was described as the 'Brent Spar of e-commerce', this combination of legal challenges, Internet attacks and media public relations stunts forced an eventual volte-face by the toy-selling company (®™ark 2000). The toy-sellers dropped their suit; since the injunction against the artists had been served their share price had lost close to 70 per cent of its value, down to US$19 per share. The defence of etoy cannot claim all the credit for this collapse; at the same time that the toy war was being conducted broader shifts in ecommerce were seeing several online companies challenged in online shopping by already established offline brand names. For the online toy-sellers etoys, the emergence of the company Toys"R"Us onto the Internet was a significant challenge. However, it is more than wishful thinking to see a connection between the hacktivism and culture jamming assault on the toy-sellers and their defeat.

The drama of the toy war, as it is now called, unfolded across a number of online and offline locations; from the courtrooms of the United States to the lego-like soldiers in the immaterial toy war platform. The resistance to viral societies, in the refusal of the artists to take the money and run, and the support they gained from an array of protestors, mark this conflict out. We can see how the actions of mass action hacktivists became closely connected to culture jammers, in the context of another refusal to bow down to the demands of globalising capitalism. The toy war lets us see mass action hacktivism in its broader protest context.

Satirical performance

Satirical performance is another way of seeing culture jamming in hacktivism and it seeks to re-appropriate the notion of performance and return an element of the dramatic to its now largely commodified meaning. Such an aim can be seen in the names of groups such as the Electronic Disturbance *Theatre* and the actions of such groups as the *Yes Men* with their satirical attacks upon the ethos of the World Trade Organisation. The performative element of hacktivist actions is designed to parody and provoke to the extent that it becomes more difficult to gloss over the political point being made.

These approaches undermine the passive reception of viral times. As already argued, direct online action consciously eschews the technical methods that would allow one single skilled hacker to cause disruption, in favour of technically unsophisticated but labour-intensive actions that require mass solidarity. Satirical performances, meanwhile, are in keeping with Baudrillard's claim that: 'The symbolic consists precisely in breaching the univocality of the "message," in restoring the ambivalence of meaning and in demolishing in the same stroke the agency of code' (Baudrillard 1981: 183). It will be useful to look at some specific examples of this promotion of ambivalence and the destruction of code.

> ®™ark felt it had to offer, perceptually if not actually, an alternative to the endless flow of bounty provided by the stock market. Much as the National Endowment for the Arts, even with its slim offerings, provided the illusion of an alternative to corporate systems – an illusion more important than the actual sums (and which has now vanished, along with the NEA's influence) – ®™ark hoped to provide a similar illusory but conceptually powerful alternative to the 'bottom line' of corporate power.
>
> (®™ark 1998a)

®™ark tends to concentrate upon satirical performance by imitating stock market models. Typical examples of their work include the setting up of a website entitled Voteauction.com. This was a website purporting to buy votes from people to highlight the democratic deficit in the United States. Other projects involved setting up a fake WTO site in order to satirise the organisation's aggressive free trade stance. The group also funded the Barbie Liberation Organisation which switched the voice boxes in 300 Talking Barbie dolls and Talking GI Joe dolls during the 1989 Christmas period to highlight the issue of gender stereotyping in children's toys.

®™ark's projects are designed with four key elements: worker, sponsor, product and idea. '®™ark is a system of workers, ideas, and money whose function is to encourage the intelligent sabotage of mass-produced items . . . ®™ark is essentially a matchmaker and bank, helping groups or individuals fund sabotage projects' (®™ark 1997). With its aim of 'intelligent sabotage' the group manifests aspects of the original conception of the 'hack' but by focusing such sabotage against mass-produced items, and by extension the system that produces them, it is overtly and intrinsically political. This politics extended dramatically into the anti-globalisation movement with the development of ®™ark's spoof-WTO site and then the extension of that with spoof talks given by the Yes Men, who act as if they come from the WTO. Satirical performance and culture jamming work against the invasion of spectacular commodity values throughout society. ®™ark recognises the mutually reinforcing effects of both the narcotic media and a social environment saturated with consumption. They refer to the way in which aesthetics have been transformed by corporate capitalism into a commodity-based *anaesthetic*.

To counter such effects, ®™ark borrows the term 'curation' from the world of art. Curates is used in the sense of 'influences' and describes (in a fashion we shall shortly see is very similar to Hardt and Negri's notion of bio-politics) the way in which daily life becomes inseparable from the pervasive and invasive commercial influence of advertisements, consumer brands and so on (®™ark 1998b). ®™ark sets itself up in direct opposition to the viral society's tendency to conceive of people as merely consumerist input mechanisms. In this sense, it is also firmly located within struggles against new capitalist social forms. ®™ark promotes the notion of citizens as performers rather than merely consumers. The activities of EDT share certain satirical elements of ®™ark but are also frequently subversive in a much more direct, performance-oriented fashion.

®™ark perceive a wellspring of potential radical opposition to commercial values and build upon it through the promotion of its various projects. When theorists such as Lash talk in terms of immanent communicational processes and informational performativity subordinated for commercial values, ®™ark attempt to re-engineer such qualities in subversive formats (Lash 2002). The Electronic Disturbance Theatre (EDT) adopts similar tactics and with their idiosyncratic emphasis upon performance and their novel form of a *politics of magic realism*. Here we rejoin the main currents of hacktivism and see, just as with the toy war, how culture jamming and hacktivism swim in the currents of the anti-globalisation movement.

> The Zapatistas use the politics of a magical realism that allows them to create these spaces of invention, intervention, and to allow the worldwide networks to witness the struggle they face daily. It was the acceptance of digital space by the Zapatistas in 12 days that created the very heart of this magical realism as information war. It was this extraordinary understanding of electronic culture which allowed the Zapatistas on 1 January, 1994, one minute after midnight just as (NAFTA) a Free Trade Agreement between Canada, USA, and Mexico went into effect – to jump into the electronic fabric, so to speak, faster than the speed of light. Within minutes people around the world had received emails from the first declaration from the Lacandona Jungle. The next day the autonomous Zapatista zones appeared all over the Internet. It was considered by the *New York Times* as the first post-modern revolution. The American intelligence community called it the first act of social net war. Remember, that this social net war was based on the simple use of email and nothing more . . . gestures can be very simple and yet create deep changes in the structures of the command and control societies that neo-liberalism agenda, like NAFTA, represent.
>
> (Dominguez cited in Fusco 1999)[1]

As we have seen, traditional forms of civil disobedience such as peaceful sit-ins have been transformed in cyberspace. What we have so far not emphasised is that some hacktivists make strong connections within their hacks to satirical performance. For example, in EDT's FloodNet DDOS attacks there is a performance element. Normally, when an unobtainable request is made on the Internet for a particular webpage the 404 error message informing the user of its unavailability comes up on the user's screen. EDT turned this technical 404 feature into an a form of artistic protest:

> We ask President Zedillo's server or the Pentagon's web server 'Where is human rights in your server?' The server then responds 'Human rights not found on this server'. . . . This use of the 'not

found' system . . . is a well known gesture among the net art communities. EDT just re-focused the 404 function towards a political gesture.

(Dominguez cited in Fusco 1999)

It is here that EDT joins classic mass action hacktivism with culture jamming; the simultaneous distributed denial of service assault on a political target with an artistic intervention that feeds back to each individual hacktivist a symbolic confirmation of why this target deserved attention. The lack of physical space in which to meet is compensated for by the binding empathy created by the positive fallout from the disturbance effects of online actions: 'The FloodNet gesture allows the social flow of command and control to be seen directly – the communities themselves can see the flow of power in a highly transparent manner' (Dominguez cited in Fusco 1999). The political questioning of this flow of power is reinforced by the fact that the point being made occurs in the form of the creative, hacked, quality of the 404 file message.

Finding performance within one of the foundation hacks of mass action hacktivism, the FloodNet, reminds us that culture jamming's obsession with signs and symbols is also an obsession with the times of anti-globalisation. We can see how hacktivism reaches out to and is affected by other elements of popular protest, that are themselves all shifting around and developing within the powerful political currents of the anti-globalisation movement. Culture jamming reminds us of the central connections of mass action hacktivism to anti-globalisation.

Bad technology means good politics

Mass action hacktivism locates online direct action firmly in relationship to the anti-globalisation movement. The importance of the Zapatista struggle to mass action's birth and self-conception, as well as the selection of targets such as the WTO, all mark mass action hacktivism as part of this late twentieth and early twenty-first-century material-isation of protest. In addition, the close connection to culture jamming, a key component of recent protests, shows hacktivism's connections to the history of social movements and protest. Yet we should not forget the roles played by viral times and the hacking community. These both form vital contexts for mass action hacktivism.

The characteristic of mass action as a trend in hacktivism is the attempt to generate a mass form of online protest, with mass being understood as a mass of individuals. Only by generating popular, collective will for change, mass action seems to be saying, will change be possible. The 'mass' of mass action hacktivism cannot be the mass generation of packets of information through automation, something so easily done in the immaterial world of cyberspace. Rather it must be the force of many people, embodied in the offline world, that gives a mass action legitimacy and political force. Dominguez claims: 'All we are doing is creating the unbearable weight of human beings in a digital way' (cited in Meikle 2002: 142).

Humans have no weight, bearable or unbearable, in cyberspace. Human weight must be re-embodied if it is to exist virtually. This commitment to embodiment, against the very nature of cyberspace, marks mass action hacktivism as the use of impure and imperfect informational technologies for political reasons. The first major trend of hacktivism lies here, in the marrying of mass, embodied, social movement protest techniques to the immaterial, bodiless, informational realm to produce a strange techno-politics; a techno-politics in which the impairment of technology is the path to unimpaired social change.

5   Digitally correct hacktivism
The purity of informational politics

The difference between hacktivists

Ricardo Dominguez tells the story this way.

The Electronic Disturbance Theatre, of which he was/is a member, was running a year long performance of online activism in support of the Zapatistas. This consisted of running FloodNet (as described in Chapter 4) from a number of places at different times; sometimes these were art conferences or events. The final action was to begin on 9 September, launched at the Ars Electronica event in Linz Austria. Three different opponents emerged to try to prevent this final FloodNet.

First, Ricardo was rung at 7.32 a.m. on the morning of the 9th and a voice speaking Spanish-Mexican stated: 'We know who you are. We know where you are at. We know where your family is. We are watching you. Do not go downstairs. Do not make your presentation. Because you know what the situation is. This is not a game.' No one ever carried out these threats or admitted making them. Second, during the FloodNet the US military launched the first known counter-cyberwar action by blocking FloodNet's actions with a targeted attack program. Intimidation and state countermeasures might be expected, but the third opponents were other counterculturalists, hackers at the Ars Electronica event. They confronted Ricardo and compatriot Stefen Wray the day before and then on the day this particular FloodNet was to be launched. These hackers argued:

> FloodNet is both ineffective due to the upstream cache and pure evil, since it represents an abuse of the network. Even if the load was to take down a server (ignoring the free speech implications for a moment, free speech you want for yourself but deny to those with

whom you disagree), you would not only impact communications with the target site, but also to those around it. FloodNet is *unacceptable* network abuse. As bad as spam, if not worse.

(EDT 1998)

After listening to such arguments from fellow-hackers Ricardo usually delivers the punchline: 'This was the first time I had heard that bandwidth rights were more important than human rights.' He nearly always gets a laugh and nodding support from his audiences. Sadly, he and his audience are, from at least one perspective, wrong.

We may examine Dominguez's position by asking: In what way can bandwidth (or more broadly understood, digital) rights be something other than human rights? Dominguez counterposes the rights and needs of Zapatista communities – poor peasant and indigenous peoples fighting back against colonialism in the context of neo-liberal globalisation – to the rights and needs of cyberspace-users. He rhetorically defeats the hackers who criticised EDT's FloodNet by opposing 'unacceptable network abuse' to 'unacceptable human abuse'; he wins this argument because most of us are still sensible enough to care more about humans than computers. With intelligence, Dominguez ensures his audiences see the world as he does; networks are tools that can be used for political purposes, they are not the owners of rights themselves. However, the hackers Dominguez disagrees with were asserting something different to Dominguez's characterisation of them. They were asserting a different set of human rights: not rights *for* networked computers but the rights *of* humans to free flows of information; not of conferring rights on inanimate objects but on what those objects offer humans. Another assertion of this rejection of digital rights versus human rights is put by one of Dominguez's compadres in EDT, Stefan Wray. He characterised the debate in this way, 'some whom call themselves hackers have criticized the FloodNet project because one of the things they allege it does is block bandwidth. This view can be said to be a digitally correct position' (Wray 1998). Like Dominguez, Wray is not praising politicised hackers here but offering the implicit condemnation of their concern for bandwidth over human rights. Yet his condemnation removes any politics from these hackers. Wray interprets their position as valuing something non-human over the human. We can interrogate this stance, we can take digitally correct hackers more seriously and explore their hacktivism. We can try to see if digital rights are also human rights.

This does not mean we have to counterpose the rights of those in the overdeveloped world to free flows of information to the rights of poor indigenous peoples in the Mexican mountains to food, education, health and personal security. To establish the potential importance of digitally correct hacktivism we shall begin with the Zaptistas. This example will allow us to see how free flows of information can be a human right of importance to all repressed peoples and not just to the already privileged. It will also remind us that the anti-globalisation movement forms a context for digitally correct hacktivism. From this demonstration, we will explore digitally correct hacktivism in its own terms. In doing this, we will be defining and exploring the second theme of hacktivism; we have seen mass virtual activism, now we will see the informational politics of hacktivists.

The Zapatistas and information

Information is key to the Zapatista struggle, as indicated by the title of the 2001 collection of Subcomandante Marcos's writings, *Our Word is Our Weapon* (Marcos 2001). It has become close to a cliché to argue that information and its grassroots distribution has been an important weapon for the Zapatistas. But this cliché, at least, remains a powerful and important political story for the information age. We considered the Zapatistas when we discussed the context of protest for hacktivism (Chapter 3); here we will focus on the role of information in that struggle.

Harry Cleaver was one of the first to outline this role, though he was soon joined by less Zapatista-friendly observers in confirming the importance of information, such as the Rand Corporation's researchers David Ronfeldt and John Arquilla (Cleaver 1998; Ronfeldt *et al.* 1998). Following the initial attempt by the Zapatistas to occupy towns in the Chiapas region, they retreated to the mountains and continued their struggle by constructing autonomous communities and agitating for social change. It became clear early on that the Zapatista National Liberation Army (EZLN) would be no match in open battle for the Mexican Army and, save for some isolated if violent instances, military conflict soon de-escalated to what the military call 'low-intensity warfare', which can perhaps be more accurately called a terror campaign against the insurgent communities. The Zapatistas were penned into inaccessible jungle and mountain regions, under constant pressure from the military. People supporting them were subject to harassment and assault. A key part of the response of the Zapatista was to spread information.

The Zapatistas made proclamations, often read and distributed through the idiosyncratic and powerful writing style of Subcomandante Marcos, offered analyses, challenged official versions, called for help, announced news and, in general, produced and encouraged production of information about their struggle. The Internet provided a key focus for this strategy as it offers far easier distribution and greater control than normal media channels. The Internet both short-circuits censorship – once information is loose in cyberspace it can be easily replicated and spread – and offers greater access – the grassroots of Zapatista organisations could post their own information with little limit on the amount they could post. The uneven distribution of access to the Internet could be overcome through the printing of net-based information to be passed around and by the access given by universities world-wide to their students, who played a key role both in posting and distributing information. Cleaver makes the point,

> given the obvious bias and incompleteness in . . . [mass media] reporting, those circulating material on the Net informally adopt the practice of posting *everything* available. As a result, those who have tapped the Net for their organising around the issues of the Zapatista struggle, and the movement for democracy in Mexico more generally, have been far better informed and far more able to shape critical assessments of any given event than the consumers of a limited sampling of mass media.
>
> (Cleaver 1998: 85)

And lest this be thought to be a biased view, that holding the mass media in contempt is a principled left-wing position, a similar assessment has been forthcoming from the, widely believed to be right-leaning, Rand Corporation. After pointing out that the Mexican government twice stopped what seemed, at the time, to be successful military initiatives in order to agree to negotiations, Ronfeldt and Arquilla argue that these turnabouts were in some ways the result of information actions, such as those Cleaver mentions.

> What led President Salinas, and later Zedillo, to halt military operations and agree to dialogue and negotiations? Varied propositions have been raised to explain their decisions. . . . Our analysis,

however, is that in both instances the transnationalist activist netwar – particularly the information operations stemming from it – was a key contributing factor. It lay behind many of the other explanations, including arousing media attention and alarming foreign investors. This activism was made possible by networking capabilities that had emerged only recently as a result of the information revolution.

(Ronfeldt and Arquilla 2001a)

Between these two accounts we see that it is information and the ability of one technology, the Internet, to spread information that has played a key role in the Zapatista struggle. The ability to spread information and from this to generate support and international pressure, which is applied both locally in Chiapas with people visiting for conferences or to be observers and internationally through demonstrations and support groups, has been crucial in the survival of the Zapatistas and their partial victories. We should not understand this as a disembodied victory for the Internet, as if somehow the wires, computers and protocols that make up the Internet took up the Zapatista struggle. Rather it reflects the use of various forms of communication technologies by activists among which the Internet has been crucial. We can see this by reflecting on the question: How do Zapatista communiqués reach the outside world, crafted as they are in the forbidding reaches of the Lacandon Jungle within communities besieged by the Mexican military? Here is an explanation, referring to a collection of Subcomandante Marcos's writing,

This book, a testimony to the power of the word, is scripted in the impossible silence of the Lacandon Jungle. Segment by segment, it is passed secretly from hand to hand, galloped inside a saddle satchel, hidden in a cyclist's bag, slipped into a backpack, or perhaps thrust inside a sack of beans, then propped in the back of an open truck, crammed with indigenous villagers who make the hours-long journey to the closest market, or doctor, and our messenger to a contact person with Internet access. Up on Dyckman Street, where Manhattan Island narrows to a close between the Hudson and Harlem Rivers . . . Greg Ruggiero surfs the net. An editor, activist and Zapatista to the core, he connects to the various websites where the latest translations of Subcomandante Marcos's communiqués reach him, and millions of others worldwide.

(De León 2001: xxiii)

There are two crucial points in this account. First, the Internet is not disembodied. People have to write and then somehow ensure that writing is published in some form. When the writing comes from a besieged community that is in revolt then individuals must take personal risks to make sure information is spread. Second, once information reaches the Internet it explodes. In this account, the broadcast of information is fragile until it reaches the Internet at which point it becomes robust. Once free to play in cyberspace the communiqués of the Zapatistas are as near to impossible to censor as is possible.

It is the infrastructure of the net itself that enables some of these possibilities. Email, by its technical nature, is easily copied and passed on. Information on the Internet is, by technical definition, already global (in the sense that nearly anyone in the world with access to the Internet can gain access to information on it). The Internet dramatically reduces the barriers to both producing and distributing information. All such changes brought by the Internet are the result of humans constructing technologies in the context of their own social and political interests (Jordan 1999a). For example, email was first introduced as a hack because an engineer felt it worthwhile; it was simply added onto communication protocols for sharing information on the Internet's predecessor Arpanet (Hafner and Lyon 1996). Many cybercultures were introduced into the Internet from pre-existing grassroots networks, such as the worldwide electronic bulletin board system Fidonet. Technologies that we use today are formed according to social values that become embedded in the technology, and so may seem to us asocial technical objects. We, in turn, alter and deform these objects, creating new ones. The point about the technical infrastructure of the Internet is not that it shows that technology determines social communication. Rather, it points to the social meaning of Internet technology and the fragility of these meanings. The infrastructure of the Internet could be remoulded into different forms according to different values; we could come to see different social meanings of the Internet as normal. It is the politico-technological nature of the Internet's infrastructure that made much of the Zapatista 'netwar' possible and that infrastructure cannot be taken for granted.

An example will help here and we can draw from outside hacktivism for this. Microsoft is well known as the provider of software that runs over 90 per cent of all personal computers and the applications package (Office) run by similar percentages of people. It has also developed a strategy and set of technologies called .Net to embrace the Internet.

These include secure trading, languages for software development, means of integrating existing languages, means of sharing personal information securely and more. Many feel this strategy is the embrace of the boa constrictor just before it swallows you, crushing your bones to make you more easily digested. *Cnet* technology correspondent Gary Hein bluntly argued: 'Microsoft.Net can be summarized in one simple statement: Microsoft is building an Internet monopoly' (Hein 2001). Many feel the Internet is impervious to such monopolisation but that remains to be seen. The Microsoft strategy at least opens the possibility of a Microsoft monopoly extending from the desktop into cyberspace. Such a monopoly may not deliver control over the content of the Internet to Microsoft, just as Microsoft's control over word-processing software does not prevent me writing this paragraph. Yet it remains an example of the fragility of the infrastructure of the Internet.

A second example is the claim that the Internet subverts national censorship. As noted already, once information is loose in cyberspace then it is available globally, it subverts national boundaries. But several nation-states have reacted to this by constructing national firewalls. These are filtering mechanisms that block access to certain sites on the Internet. The most often mentioned nations are China and Singapore but there are others. This means that, for example, in China you often cannot access BBC.co.uk, the British public broadcaster's site, or CNN.com, the American-based news site. The infrastructure of the Internet is here tampered with to control access to information on a national basis.

We can now see both the use of the Internet in the struggle for human rights and the fragility of the infrastructure that has, in the past, supported such struggles. What these examples show us is that it is not a question of human rights versus bandwidth rights but of different types of human rights. In one sense, the human rights supported by organisations such as Electronic Disturbance Theatre are simply that, a focus on the rights of humans to various things like housing, food and so on. What has been called bandwidth rights, but should perhaps be more properly called digital rights, is a specific form of human right; the right to information. This means the opposition is not between human and non-human rights but different sorts of human rights.

The digitally correct hacktivist concentrates on human rights but of a particular sort; in this sense Wray and Dominguez are wrong to imply digitally correct hacktivists aim at rights for machines rather than rights for humans. Rather, it is the human right to secure access to information, usually incarnated as secure, private access to the Internet. This is a right-in-itself, the right to know what is happening to one's community and to one's world, but it can also be thought of as something like an indirect right. It is a politics that is often useful in serving other political ideals. We can return to the use of the Internet in the Zapatista struggle to understand this. The primary demands of the Zapatistas are for health, welfare and citizenship rights. Healthier food, better access to education and health services, greater cultural recognition and autonomy: these would all make concrete changes in the lives of Zapatista communities. In this struggle, the Internet functions as a medium through which the demands for these rights and the struggles around these rights can be communicated. Information rights appear here as almost a second political order, serving the 'first order' rights to health, welfare and full citizenship. It means digitally correct hacktivists can end up producing tools that are widely used and which ensure access to information, but which can be used by many different political groups of very different political persuasions.

We now have an initial understanding of digitally correct hacktivism and some of the issues surrounding it. To explore these we will take up the hacktivist group Cult of the Dead Cow and look at two case studies: peek-a-booty and Back Orifice. In both these cases we will see digitally correct hacktivism at work. Finally, we will push the discussion of digitally correct hacktivism to a conclusion by exploring arguments between the digitally correct and mass action hacktivists.

Cult of the Dead Cow

The Cult of the Dead Cow (CDC) have been around since the mid-1980s (an unusual degree of longevity in terms of the hacker community). It began as a t-files, or text-files group, passing rants, fiction and technology plans around as part of the then bulletin board-based system of computer communication called Fidonet (Jordan 1999a: 38–9). Over the years and changes of both personnel and surrounding technologies, CDC became known as a hacking group and, then, as a hacktivist group. They achieved an underground, and overground, fame due to both their hacking/hacktivist tools and their willingness to discuss their views publicly. They stand as one of the clearest examples of a group committed to the principles of digitally correct hacktivism. This can be seen in their, now often-quoted, response to the Electrohippies justification for their denial of service strike against networks serving the 1999 WTO conference in Seattle. CDC argued:

> Denial of Service attacks are a violation of the First Amendment, and of the freedoms of expression and assembly. No rationale, even in the service of the highest ideals, makes them anything other than what they are – illegal, unethical, and uncivil. One does not make a better point in a public forum by shouting down one's opponent. Say something more intelligent or observe your opponents' technology and leverage your assets against them in creative and legal ways. . . . Hacktivism is about using more eloquent arguments – whether of code or words – to construct a more perfect system. One does not become a hacktivist merely by inserting an 'h' in front of the word activist or by looking backward to paradigms associated with industrial organization.
>
> (Ruffin 2000)

Digitally correct hacktivism – focused on the rights of all to information – here confronts mass, anti-globalisation hacktivism. The ethical ground set by CDC's Foreign Minister Oxblood Ruffin is firmly that of free flows of information; cyberspace allows all views to be heard, shouting down makes no sense in virtual lands. Another CDC member, Count Zero, defines hacktivism in the same way:

> focusing on empowering the people . . . with the TOOLS of hacktivism . . . making the WORLD know about the injustices and human rights abuses . . . in other words, getting the FLOW of INFORMATION pumpin' around the globe . . . UNIMPEDED and UNCENSORED . . . THAT's hacktivism'.
>
> (Count Zero 1999)

CDC like most activist groupings, or in the larger sense like social movements, is not a straightforwardly discrete and hierarchical organisation, but is a loose network of individuals, ideas and actions. One example demonstrates this. In 1999, CDC announced that a group called Hacktivismo had been formed. This group set about exploring ways of preventing censorship of the Internet, in particular focusing on firewalls or censoring mechanisms put in place by national governments. From the start the FAQ (frequently asked questions) and press release tried to make it clear that CDC and Hacktivismo were different groups, though slightly confusingly Hacktivismo was also described as a 'special operations group' of CDC. By early 2002, Hacktivismo was being described as 'an international cadre of hackers founded by the CDC's Oxblood Ruffin' (Ruffin 2002) in a press release that then announced the project had been taken over from Hacktivismo by its lead software designer Paul Baranowski (also known as Drunken Master) who had left Hacktivismo. The rationale for this move was that the project was going too slowly while people tried to work on it in their spare time, so Drunken Master took over the project totally as he had quit his job to work on it full time. From being either a sub-group or separate group of CDC, peek-a-booty became a project under the control of one person. Through all this the basic project, described below, stayed the same, retaining the same significance for hacktivists. This is an example of the difficulty of tracing individuals and groups, given the fluid nature of hacker identities and commitments, but it shows the corresponding solidity of hacktivist projects. When discussing digitally correct hacktivism, it is projects that are key not groups or individuals.

To pursue the human rights embodied by digitally correct hacktivists we will now turn to two case studies of projects. The first is peek-a-booty. The advantage of peek-a-booty is that it demonstrates more clearly than any other project the particular politics and morality of digitally correct hacktivism. However, it also suffers from a significant weakness in that it is, at the time of writing, still a project that has been demonstrated but not released. It even made *Wired* magazine's Top 10 Vapourware projects for 2001; vapourware being software that is announced but never delivered. Nevertheless we have chosen peek-a-booty as an example because it is a serious project, with coding that is conducted and demonstrated; its vapourware status also demonstrates the fragility of software production, which is as true of hacktivist projects as of any other. The second case study complicates and extends the picture produced by peek-a-booty, and is an examination of Back Orifice. This tool extends discussion of hacktivism into grey areas of cracking and touches on issues of open source and free software, connecting digitally correct hacktivism to the hacking community. It was announced by CDC, its organisers, as a major moment in hacktivism, yet it has all the hallmarks of a cracking tool. How such a piece of software can be considered political opens up some of the theoretical complexities raised by hacktivism.

Peek-a-booty and Back Orifice mark distinct yet linked moments of hacktivism. They both swirl around CDC but are not contained or

defined by CDC's involvement. After we have explored these case
studies, we will assess digitally correct hacktivism and the human right
to information.

Peek-a-booty

On 26 February 2002 a link was pasted as the lead item on the peek-a-
booty website (www.peek-a-booty.org), a link to an 'awesome' article
about China and the Internet. The article explored the ways in which
US corporations have colluded with Chinese state officials to install
censoring and surveillance mechanisms into the Chinese networks that
connect to the Internet. The article reported that Cisco, makers of
hardware that organises the distribution of information through the
Internet (routers), devised specific technologies to meet government
demands to be able to block and monitor anyone accessing the Internet
from China. It also reported that Yahoo! had allowed real-time
censorship of chat rooms and blocked searches for such keywords as
'Taiwan independence' or 'Falun Gong' or 'China democracy'. The
interest of this report for peek-a-booty and digitally correct hacktivism
is that it establishes clearly who the enemy is: state-sponsored censorship
and surveillance of the Internet (Gutman 2002).

One widespread interpretation of the Internet is that this fear of
censorship is a misunderstanding. The Internet has been understood
as uncensorable; for example, online activist and technologist John
Gilmore claimed 'the Internet treats censorship as damage, it routes
around it'. It is believed by many that a technology which both sends
messages via a decentred network and lowers dramatically the costs of
producing and distributing information, means censorship becomes
extremely difficult. On the one hand, the Internet sends information
through networks which can route different parts of a message through
different parts of the network. This means that even if one part of
the network is blocked, other parts will pass the message on, thereby
defeating any blocks on network points. On the other hand, the Internet
dramatically reduces costs of producing and distributing information
for those who can gain access to it. This means it is not as hard for
someone to place their information in the public domain on the Internet
as it is in television, radio or print media. On this basis, it is argued that
the Internet by its very technical and economic nature will ensure information proliferates to anyone who can gain access. But this argument,
while it grasps some points about the Internet, is flawed.

First, it is important not to go overboard in rejecting this type of argument. The Internet does often route around censorship. If someone closes one site down and that site is recreated (because it is easy to copy and send the files) elsewhere, particularly elsewhere in the world with different legal jurisdiction, then it is hard to prevent those accessing the Internet from seeing the information on that site. When Italian magistrates closed down the hacktivist site 'Netstrike', it was soon recreated elsewhere beyond the reach of Italian law. Moreover, a package of files was created allowing anyone able to host a website to recreate the Netstrike site. The anti-McDonald's website, McSpotlight, was initially located on computers in the Netherlands, despite many British workers being involved in its creation, because it was believed the Netherlands provided a more permissive legal system for such a site (Meikle 2002: 75–81).

In many ways the Internet can avoid censorship or at least ensure a multiplicity of views are heard, rather than those deemed legitimate by major state or corporate bodies. However, in other ways this is not so. First and foremost, the Internet is both decentred and centred. Censorship has always been possible at the centre of the Internet, though there are few cases of such censorship. The Internet is centralised because it uses a translation between numbers and letters to define the location of Internet resources. When someone types www.open.ac.uk into their browser then these letters are automatically translated into numbers such as 192.177.02.5, which the Internet's routers and computers then use to identify the resource being requested. This allows people to work mainly with letters and computers with numbers, each playing to their respective strengths. However, a central database is also needed to ensure numbers and letters match each other. This database was and remains a potential centring mechanism and source of censorship. For example, during the toy war when the toy-sellers obtained an injunction against the artists, it was the body that administers this central database which removed them from the Internet.

There are less centralised forms of surveillance as well. Web pages download 'cookies' that track browsing histories. 'Spyware' that keeps track of someone's online habits is often unknowingly installed. Logs of anyone's online adventures are kept by most ISPs and can be used to trace someone's virtual movements. Most email is sent as open, plain text that can be read by anyone with the skill and motivation. Companies and nation-states can put barriers to access to the Internet that block certain places on the Internet from those who are within the corporation or nation-state.

Digitally correct hacktivists know that the Internet is censorable, they know that it is a battle over the nature of technological objects and the values those objects are created with. It is a battle over the technical infrastructure of the Internet and the social values that can be embedded within this infrastructure. To enable free flows of information in the Internet, digitally correct hacktivists seek to imbue the Internet's technological infrastructure with the values of freedom of information. It is the central battle for these hacktivists.

Peek-a-booty has the potential to be an important weapon in this battle. It engages in the high stakes of national and international politics through the organised expertise of guerrilla or resistance technologists. While the purpose of peek-a-booty is not hard to explain – resist nation-states' attempts to censor the Internet – the way politics is embedded in technologies is less clear. To understand peek-a-booty's significance it is important to spend some time exploring its technical nature. We can avoid an overly long excursion into software design and engineering by following the presentation given by peek-a-booty developers to the conference *Codecon* in Februrary 2002. In this presentation, the developers, Paul Baranowski and Joey DeVilla, explored the main features of peek-a-booty in four parts, each of which is primarily politico-technical in nature: distributed, steganography, anonymous connection and minimal discovery. A brief outline of all four will offer an overview of peek-a-booty (Baranowski 2002). Following this it will be important to outline a fifth aspect of peek-a-booty, one that can be considered primarily politico-organisational.

Distributed

Peek-a-booty is a network of computers communicating with each other. Each point at which two, or more, computers' connections cross (usually itself another computer) is called a node. On networks nodes have essentially two ways of operating; either being a client that is served information from elsewhere or being a server that stores and provides information when asked. If the server is centralised then a central point allows clear organisation, and this is the way many networks operate, with clients requesting their information from one primary point. However, if each node is simultaneously a client and a server then the network is a distributed one, on which there is no central point but instead a rapidly circulating series of messages, handled by different nodes on the network. Peek-a-booty is a distributed network and the reasons for this type of technical infrastructure are a combination of politico-technological and legal.

The politico-techonological reason is that distributed networks, though they are more complex, are harder to shut down. A centralised network only needs it central server to be shut down and the network collapses; the clients are useless in network terms without their server. But if all nodes are clients and servers then only shutting down the majority of nodes will shut down the network. Shutting down some nodes will shut down a portion of the network but the remainder will continue to function. While this looks like a technical argument, it is a concern only if a network needs to be designed with a deliberate attack in mind. If someone expects the network they are designing to be the target of sustained attempts to disable it then it is the social and political nature of the network that demands it be robust against attacks. In the case of peek-a-booty, its aim of disturbing censorship of the Internet means it can expect to be the target of attack and being distributed therefore has important advantages.

The legal reasons for choosing a distributed architecture are closely related to these, as legally shutting down a centralised network only requires locating whoever is legally responsible for the central server, defining what jurisdiction this person(s) exists under and then prosecuting them. However, shutting down a distributed network using legal means involves defining the responsible person and relevant jurisdiction for each node and then prosecuting each. Given that nodes will have different legal locations – both international and inter-regional – it can become a monumental financial and temporal burden prosecuting a distributed network.

Steganography

The second component of peek-a-booty is its use of steganography. Steganography means concealing messages as something innocuous. Peek-a-booty needs something like this in order to get through the firewall, if a message leaving or entering a nation can be identified by the firewall as a peek-a-booty-related message then it can be blocked. The peek-a-booty message must be passed through the national firewall but not be recognised, it must have a virtual false moustache and glasses placed on it. Again we find a politico-technological choice made here. Peek-a-booty uses secure socket layer (or SSL) protocols. These protocols define rules for a number of things provided by SSL: data encryption, server authentication, message integrity and client authentication for a TCP/IP connection. All in all, SSL hides data through encryption and it validates the servers serving the SSL request. SSL is the major vehicle for secure online financial transactions and, because of this, SSL is built into all major browsers and web servers. SSL is a technology serving the commercialisation of the Internet and it is very difficult for any national firewall to block SSL messages as this would effectively cut off that nation from the majority of e-commerce transactions. Few sites behind a national firewall that blocked SSL would be able to offer goods for sale over the Internet using secure transactions and few customers would be able to buy goods securely outside the national firewall. For commercial reasons SSL is difficult to block, even if SSL messages are carrying prohibited information rather than just buy and sell transactions.

The possibility arises that an opponent of peek-a-booty might try to break the encryption on SSL and check inside SSL packets for relevant information. It is however unlikely that any nation would acknowledge decrypting and looking inside SSL transactions because this would undermine the security of online trade. Breaking and examining the contents of SSL messages would mean seeing peoples' financial details (credit card numbers and expiry dates, for example, or passwords to stored financial details), not just peek-a-booty-related information. Any nation known to be pursuing such a course would be quickly seen as a nation destroying the fabric of e-commerce. A second reason breaking SSL is unlikely is that SSL uses reasonably strong encryption and huge amounts of SSL messages are sent. This combination means it would be very difficult, on a regular basis, to scan all SSL messages and sift out commercial from non-commercial messages. The sheer deluge of SSL messages passing through nearly all networks, combined with the difficulty of breaking any one SSL message's encryption, means that even if a nation were willing to take the commercial and international political risk of scanning SSL, it would still face a formidable technical obstacle in achieving such a task.

As with the decision in favour of a distributed versus a centralised network, the use of SSL for peek-a-booty's steganographic needs is a politico-technical one. It is a decision that assesses available steganographies and uses SSL because SSL's centrality in e-commerce means there are significant technical and political barriers to stopping peek-a-booty messages hidden within SSL messages.

Anonymity

The third component of peek-a-booty as a network is that it uses anonymous connections. The aim is to prevent anyone tracing a peek-a-booty message back to its source or to prevent mapping out all the different nodes on the peek-a-booty network. Here we draw closer to the architecture of peek-a-booty's network and begin to see what kind of a network it is. Someone connected to the Internet can make a request for information through the peek-a-booty network. Their request is passed to what is called a 'cloud' of servers. This simply means that peek-a-booty, as a network, has at its service a number of servers, each a computer connected to peek-a-booty via the Internet and each volunteered by its owner. To become part of the peek-a-booty network a computer's controller simply downloads the peek-a-booty software and installs it. When a request reaches this cloud – this collection of volunteer servers – one particular server picks it up. The request is passed among a number of these servers, not all of them, until one server decides to go to the final destination and send back the required information. For example, if there are ten computers in the server cloud (each for the purposes of this example identified by a letter from A to J) and someone makes a request for CNN.com, then that request might go to servers A then D then F and then to CNN.com, before being returned. The key is whether each link in this chain can be identified from the other links, and so both the source and the requester identified. If this can be done then the network can be identified in order to stop the chain of communication and anyone requesting illicit information can be traced.

Peek-a-booty answers this problem in a way that means, it is claimed, all links in the chain are made anonymous to each other. The method is to make each chain through which a request is served new for each request and to randomise which links will be used. In addition, the sender and target are kept secret from the links in the chain. Each such chain is called a virtual circuit. When a request is made to a link in the chain that link (or server) has a probability of taking the request or not. These probabilities ensure that each server does not constantly take all requests, it randomises whether each server is willing to be a link in a virtual circuit. Once the server has decided it will randomly take a particular request it looks at a number that is attached to the request and adds to it a number of its own. For example, the request first arrives to the server cloud and a random number is attached to it, in this case

1, by the first server that decides to take the request, passing it then to server D which attaches number 2, to server F which attaches number 3 and finally to CNN.com. Then the request can be passed back down the chain with each link knowing where to send the request based on these numbers: F matches 3 to 2 and sends the request back to sever D, D matches 2 to 1 and sends the request back to server A and so on. In this way, each server only matches randomly generated numbers to randomly generated links. Allied to a large number of potential servers in the cloud, this hopefully creates a randomised chain for each request, and a chain in which links are anonymised from each other. Here we see the complexity that the political imperatives of peek-a-booty imposes on technological solutions or, perhaps more accurately, how political imperatives and the nature of technologies are inextricably intertwined.

Discovery

The final component of peek-a-booty's politico-technological formation is that of minimal discovery. With the previous three components all working, peek-a-booty, in theory, has achieved its aim of routing information securely through national firewalls. However, peek-a-booty's mission suggests it is likely to be subject to attack as well. Some attacks are a general hazard of operating on the Internet, such as denial of service attacks. But some attacks might be expected particularly against a network such as peek-a-booty. Techniques that have been used against other similar networks (such as that which mapped out peer-to-peer network Gnutella) might be employed by opponents of peek-a-booty. Therefore minimal discovery became the fourth component of peek-a-booty.

The Internet allows messages to be passed quickly around different nodes and these nodes must in some way identify themselves in order to receive messages intended for them and to pass messages on. To accomplish this each connection to the Internet receives a unique number, its Internet Protocol or IP number. Each node of a peek-a-booty network will have an IP number. It follows that one way of stopping peek-a-booty would be for someone to map all the computers using the peek-a-booty network then they could simply, and possibly automatically, update their firewall with peek-a-booty IP numbers, effectively blocking peek-a-booty. This is a difficult problem for peek-a-booty's designers to solve because it is essential that computers be able to find each other by using IP numbers; it is in a sense the fundamental tenet of the Internet. This requirement also goes against the fundamental direction of peer-to-peer networks, which usually wish to know all the addresses of nodes in order to know what each node contains and to route messages appropriately. To ensure that no one can map out the whole peek-a-booty network minimal discovery is being developed. This has two components.

First, messages that are not carrying data but are simply travelling around the network checking on nodes and addresses need to be limited. These can be called discovery messages as their role is to discover and map nodes on the network. As peek-a-booty is a dynamic network, it is hoped and expected that nodes will be constantly joining and leaving the network. This means that ensuring only a limited number of discovery messages will be answered by peek-a-booty nodes should provide some block on discovering all nodes at a single moment in time. With nodes leaving and joining, if the blocking of discovery messages is set at an appropriate level, then there should be no real chance of mapping the whole network. There are some possible difficulties here as discovery messages allow the network itself to know nodes and their connections so they cannot be blocked entirely. The crucial problem is the number of messages that are blocked. There is also a related problem.

If packages or discovery messages are allowed to exist over time, they can map the network over a period of time rather than trying to map it as quickly as possible. The answer here is complex and involves making each decision to receive or send on a packet by a node one based on probability. Averages for the number of messages that will be processed and the number of nodes each message will pass through have to be set. These averages determine what level of probability should be used. Without delving into the complex mathematics behind such decisions, the averages themselves are determined by the requirement of minimal discovery. And this is determined by the principle that the number of discovery-requests answered must be less than the number of new nodes joining the network. This means that no matter how many discovery-requests are made, there will always be part of the network that cannot be discovered over time because there are more nodes joining than discovery-requests being answered. In this way peek-a-booty should solve its problems with someone targeting the whole network; parts of peek-a-booty's network will always be discoverable, but the whole network will survive. What happens to the owners of the nodes that are discovered has not been clearly considered by the creators of peek-a-booty, although at their CodeCon presentation they pointed out that anyone running peek-a-booty should be willing to take the risk and then joked that they should put in the end-user licence agreement (eula) that peek-a-booty producers were 'not responsible for your death' (Baranowski 2002).

Society

Finally, in outlining peek-a-booty, we can see how having solved their politico-technological problems in producing a network that can achieve its aims, the developers and administrators of peek-a-booty will have to consider some related politico-organisational problems. This constitutes the fifth aspect of peek-a-booty that must be considered in addition to the four politico-technological aspects and refers to the organisational or social network that must accompany the computer network. All computer networks rely on or necessarily involve social or organisational networks simply to ensure the computers are connected and correctly configured. Before anyone can use peek-a-booty the computer network must be created and for anyone to go on using peek-a-booty a social or organisational network must ensure the mundane maintenance of cables, code and computers. For example, each node in the server cloud is a computer running peek-a-booty software, and that software has to be downloaded and installed. In large state or corporate entities such politico-organisational networks are likely to be determined by the existing institutional structures. Peek-a-booty, like many social movement organisations, presents a new set of potential structures.

Peek-a-booty will be spread through many of the usual Internet distribution channels: sites that download software, sites that promote similar political causes and so on. Various human rights organisations are likely to be involved in the distribution of peek-a-booty software when it becomes available. There will also be the possibility of downloading peek-a-booty from existing peek-a-booty nodes. In these ways, with the distribution powers of the Internet, peek-a-booty should be passed around to anyone wishing to use or support it. Once it is being used peek-a-booty will employ a screensaver that offers a picture of the network, showing nodes as bears with their mouths taped over or typing, which will indicate other nodes on the network and whether these are working or not. This is so that people who enrol in the peek-a-booty project can see some return and see they are part of a network. Though only a whimsical graphical representation, the bears serve the purpose all social movements have of keeping members engaged and interested. Through these means peek-a-booty hopes to reach and engage a constituency interested in promoting digital rights.

Now we can see peek-a-booty at a design stage which suggests it is both possible and nearing completion but also too early to be certain it will actually become a functioning network. We have seen four different ways in which peek-a-booty is constituted by politico-technological forms, each of which in the very nature of the technology that is developed enacts certain political principles. In peek-a-booty's case the fundamental aim is to ensure free flows of information across the Internet to people whose national governments are denying such free flows. What people choose to take securely across a national firewall with the aid of peek-a-booty is not predetermined, after all political, religious and economic information is banned by national firewalls but so are pornography, racists sites and even some sports information. Peek-a-booty will not distinguish between the information it carries and that reflects its politics. The technology allows all information banned by a firewall to pass that barrier. Peek-a-booty is the embodiment of a digitally correct politics in its treatment of all information at a basic level as information.

Peek-a-booty is not alone in this desire of digitally correct hacktivism to allow, even encourage, information to flow. Within the same year that peek-a-booty seemed to rise from the ashes as a project, that is when it passed from being vapourware to a publicly demonstrable prototype, three other projects of similar intent and even technological conception were announced or released. Two of these were from Cult of the Dead Cow, so the similar concern to peek-a-booty is unsurprising, but still their coincident emergence marks a common hacktivist desire. There is no need to detail them as we have detailed peek-a-booty but it is useful to outline briefly their politico-technological formation.

Camera/shy was released by Cult of the Dead Cow in 2002 and is a software package that hides information within digital images. Information can then be passed across national firewalls or into censored areas. It involves a web browser that hides its users' trail and incorporates automatic decrypting of encrypted images (CDC 2002). The Hacktivismo group announced in 2002 a project to create Six/Four, a virtual private nework aimed at subverting national firewalls. Six/four is the date June 4th on which thousands of demonstrators in Tiananmen Square were attacked by the Chinese state and 'The goal of The Six/Four System is to provide access to any information that is available through a public Internet service, especially HTTP'. Six/four was released in

2003 and is available from the hacktivismo website (Schachtman 2002; Hacktivismo 2003). While these two projects might seem to come from the same part of the hacktivist community, developers at the Massachusetts Institute of Technology (MIT) also produced new software which allows users to request banned pages. These pages are disguised as images, steganography again, and are passed back to the user who can decode the image (*New Scientist* 2002).

In the light of these similar projects a particular political imagination can be seen at work. We shall return to this imagination in concluding this chapter. For now we need only note a few points before turning to a less clearly political example. First, we should note the clear intermingling, the inextricable intertwining, of politics and technology. It makes no sense to separate or distinguish between the two; to reflect this the phrase 'politico-technological formation' has been used. In comparison to hacktivists employing mass virtual direct actions, digitally correct hacktivists work inside technologies, imbuing the very fabric of cyberspace with their political values. The politico-technological formations of digitally correct hacktivists *are* their political imaginations brought to life. For mass virtual direct action hacktivists, their technological formations serve their political goals. Without suggesting a hard and fast dividing line, we can perhaps see that one set of hacktivists forms their politics *in* technologies whereas another forms their politics *through* technologies.

Second, technology and politics are joined within a context of organisation and broad mass support similar to that underpinning mass virtual direct actions. The technological products of the digitally correct need distribution, and sometimes mass use, and to achieve this politico-social as well as politico-technological end networks must come into being. The emphasis may be reversed, with digitally correct hacktivists calling social networks into being because their politico-technological formations demand it, rather than as with mass action hacktivists who are primarily concerned to generate politico-social networks.

To complete the picture of digitally correct hacktivism it will be important to draw it back towards the hacking community. So far we have drawn hacktivism gradually away from this key source by examining first the separation of hacktivism from hacking, then detailing the least hacker-like of all hacktivists in mass action hacktivists. Finally, we explored in detail a digitally correct hacktivism focused on the politics of nation-states and extra-national bodies in globalising times. But the politics of information brings hacktivism closer to hacking than has hitherto been clear in these pages. To see this it will be useful to take up a second intervention involving Cult of the Dead Cow; here we meet the provocatively named 'Back Orifice'.

Back Orifice

Back Orifice (BO) is a reflection of a long-standing claim of many hackers, that they are improving computer security. Hackers do this by cracking computers, that is by finding a security vulnerability and then exploiting it and then by reporting the vulnerability. It is an often-told story of a hacker breaking into a computer and then discussing with the systems administrator of that computer how they did it, sometimes even berating the administrator for having such lax security. While this may seem strange behaviour from a burglar – sitting in your lounge room waiting for you to come home so that they can tell you the locks they have just broken are not adequate – it fits entirely with many hackers' belief that they are explorers and not criminals. Having found a vulnerability, hackers may see it as their public service to report it. Back Orifice represents a codified version of this viewpoint, as it provides an automated means of breaking into and controlling computer systems remotely. As an illicit remote-management system it makes a point about privacy by demonstrating the control over our computers, and all the information they contain, that systems administrators have. We will first explain how BO works and then explore what possible politics such a seemingly mischievous piece of software might embody.

BO, including its various versions, is an illicit remote-administration tool for Windows-based networks. It is a software package available on the Internet (see http://sourceforge.net/projects/bo2k/) that can be installed and then run. It provides a gui (graphic-user-interface) which means it allows point and click use, dramatically lowering technical barriers to the use of such software. Initially, it operates roughly like a trojan horse program. That is, a BO file is attached to another file or is imported some way or other onto a target computer, the BO file then runs itself and installs itself. It also removes the initial executing file once it is installed. The person introducing the BO trojan horse then has full systems administrator privileges on the targeted computer. That means they can look at the hard drive of the targeted machine, copy files from it, execute programs on it, even record every keystroke run on it; in short, it offers full control of the targeted machine (CERT 1998; Virus Bulletin 1998a,b). BO fundamentally compromises the security of any computer it infects, though it is currently restricted to machines and networks using Windows operating systems.

BO reflects the later generations of hackers, as discussed in Chapter 1, who can take advantage of automated tools which embody expertise; rather than having to know exactly how each vulnerability in a computer or network can be exploited, these hackers develop expertise in using other people's programs. Hackers who utilise such tools are sometimes derisively known as 'script-kiddies', which tends to mean, abusively, someone who is not really a hacker but just uses other people's expertise via a tool or script. The place of BO within the hacking community is clear. It is yet another tool available for breaking into and controlling other computers and networks. Interestingly, it has also taken on a second life as a free, open source remote administration tool, and this now overshadows BO's cracking abilities. Again, this places BO squarely within both the hacking and the wider open source movement.

There is no doubt that Cult of the Dead Cow intended BO to be a part of the hacktivist struggle. When the 2000 version (BO2K) was released at hacker conference DefCon, they explicitly called it a moment in hacktivism, as well as prefacing their demonstration of BO2K's capabilities with some calls to hackers to develop political relevance in their hacks (CDC 1999b). But where is the politics here? BO seems to be more purely a hacking tool. And this is partly true. As we will see, BO is harder to distinguish as a hacktivist rather than a hacking application than peek-a-booty is. This is as it should be: the difference between hacking and hacktivism is more amenable to analytic distinctions than practical examples. The boundary is permeable, uncertain and shifting. However, there is a difference, and BO, in the difficulty it presents in being seen as a hacktivist's tool, offers a useful case study. To see it in terms of hacktivism we can turn to CDC's political claims for BO.

The justification for the writing and release of this software was that it forced Microsoft and users of Microsoft's operating systems to face up to security issues that are normally hidden. CDC pointed out that Microsoft attacks the stealth features of Back Orifice but that Microsoft includes, as part of its Systems Management Server software, tools that also allow secret, remote access to computers. CDC's point is that all users of Microsoft-based networks are subject to exactly the surveillance that BO offers. All systems administrators, or whoever has access to the systems management software, have the same stealth capabilities as those offered by BO. The difference between the two software packages is not in what they do but that Microsoft's stealth features are highly likely to remain in the hands of those who administer a network, whereas Back Orifice is available to anyone. Distinguishing Microsoft's Systems Management Server software from BO revolves around not their different capabilities but who is likely to have access to and control of the software. How 'we' as ordinary users feel, either reassured or threatened, depends not on whether we can be secretly examined but who is doing the examining and whether we have access to the tools to return the compliment (CDC 1999a).

The politics here is one of security of access and privacy of information. CDC are pointing out to everyone that there is no security and privacy on Microsoft networks unless there have been some alterations to the network to provide these. And any such alterations will remain at the mercy of systems administrators to alter them again. This is not, on CDC's part, an attempt to paint computer systems administrators as spying power-mongers. It is rather a point about the nature of such systems and the way powers are distributed across them. Most importantly, it is a point about publicising this situation through the drama of BO. BO emerges here not just as a cracking application but as a piece of online political drama or subversive performance. BO seeks to demonstrate and publicise to all the vulnerability of their information in computer networks and does so in as dramatic a way as possible, by threatening many with illicit intrusion and by offering many the potential to conduct illicit intrusion. In this unlikely way, we see a connection between the most cracker-like moment of digitally correct hacktivism and the performative dimensions of mass action hacktivism.

BO here takes its place as a theatrical moment in digitally correct hacktivism. It attempts to play out for people the nature of their online life, with a deliberate focus on the values that inform digitally correct hacktivism; secure access to information flows. There is no denying that since its release BO has drifted far more into the cracking and open source movements, as if once its potential for drama was released through news articles and a reactive release of virus alerts about it, then the hacktivist show was over for BO. However, it is also important to see that the minutiae of how our computer networks run is the subject of digitally correct hacktivism. It also demonstrates that hacktivism is part of and yet separate from hacking and related movements like open source, and that these involve connections and relations rather than boundaries and separations. BO demonstrates to us, again, the informational focus of digitally correct hacktivism; this focus is not on the nature of individual bits of information or the politics of those using information – anyone can download and use BO whatever their politics – but on the infrastructure of information, on who gets access to what within cyberspace.

Digitally correct hacktivism

Free flows of information are at the core of digitally correct hacktivism. Whereas mass action hacktivists look to networks to do things for them, to be a place in which protest can occur just as roads are places in which demonstrations can occur, digitally correct hacktivists attempt to form the nature of the roads and passages of cyberspace. In doing this they generate actions directly focused on the codes that make cyberspace the place it is.

Though digitally correct hacktivists also draw on the anti-globalisation movement, it is clear they are closely connected to the hacking community and inspired by viral times. The core ethical drive of digitally correct hacktivism is taken directly from hacking but has been revived and politicised. The techniques of digitally correct hacktivism, the forming of small teams of experts to hothouse software in an open collaborative environment, is drawn from hacking (and other forms of software production). The audience is other hackers, allowing digitally correct hacktivists to also revel in the peer-recognition produced by creating a good hack, a recognition fundamentally important to the hacking community (Taylor 1999). But the impact of viral times is also present. Digitally correct hacktivists watch the flows of information becoming subjected to the regulatory and corporate demands of informational capitalism, they see the resistances posed by elements of the anti-globalisation movement, and they have generated a politicisation of hacking. However close to hacking digitally correct hacktivism can be, it is also a significant change.

The digitally correct aim for efficient technologies and within those technologies articulate their politics. It is in the software code and its functions that information will be freed. It is in the details of coded products, as we saw with peek-a-booty, that digital hacktivism lives its politics. This is in marked contrast to mass action hacktivism, whose impaired technology denies the powers of cyberspace that, in a general sense, are the prized object of digitally correct hacktivism. This difference creates both agreements and disagreements between the two strands. Mass action hacktivists, like all cyberspace users, can benefit greatly from the efforts of the digitally correct, and the digitally correct can gain a stronger political context from mass action for their efforts. But at the same time, and as we saw when discussing hacker objections to EDT's FloodNet, digitally correct hacktivists at times object to mass action's use of bandwidth and emphasis on closing down enemies in cyberspace. We have earlier quoted CDC member Oxblood Ruffin's objection to the ehippies' running of the Seattle WTO virtual sit-in, but it is worth remembering his words: 'No rationale, even in the service of the highest ideals, makes them anything than what they are – illegal, unethical, and uncivil. One does not make a better point in a public forum by shouting down one's opponent' (Ruffin 2000).

We have now before us the two key streams of hacktivism. Digitally correct hacktivists create purist technologies for an informational politics. Mass action hacktivists create impure technologies for a mass politics. We shall now turn to explore the implications and significance of hacktivism. And, after this chapter, it will be no surprise that we need to turn back to the hacking community in order to grasp one of the shifts in digital culture that hacktivism has brought.

6 Men in the matrix
Informational intimacy

Introduction

Hacktivism breaks down into two broad streams of actions:

1 Mass virtual direct actions, which use cyberspatial technologies of limited potential in order to re-embody virtual actions.
2 Digitally correct actions, which defend and extend the peculiar powers cyberspace creates.

These streams interact and conflict. They should not be taken as entirely separate entities but as trends or currents within the whole hacktivist movement. On this basis we will examine the significance of hacktivism, both in shifts within digital cultures and within politics more broadly. First we will explore shifts within hardcore digital cultures. Discussion here focuses mainly on the digital culture closest to hacktivism – hacking – but offers conclusions that have relevance to notions of bodies and embodiment in hacking and hacktivism, drawing upon hacking's historical gender bias. Second, in Chapter 7, we will extend our analysis from its close engagement with digital cultures to the broader political significance of hacktivism. We will show how hacktivism has significance not only for digital cultures but more broadly for the politics and cultures of viral, informational times. Together these two chapters will establish some of the significant changes underway within hacktivism within the context of globalisation politics and immaterial, informational commodities.

To see the effects of hacktivism within virtuality, we need first to re-examine the account of hacking provided in earlier chapters. This will re-establish our understanding of the potential within hacktivism for a regressive politics associated with hacking. This provides an important contextualisation for our exploration of the more radical features of hacktivism. Building upon Turkle's category of male tendency towards the hard mastery of technological objects, and using cyberpunk fiction as a useful additional conceptual resource, we address hacking's various conformist stereotypically masculine elements. Of particular interest is hacking's periodically disturbing over-identification with technical means over ends and a love of systems for their own sake. We will see in this desire for mastery, this obsession with means over ends, a regressive conception of masculinity that runs through hacking. Despite their shared etymological roots, this chapter contrasts hacktivism's radical political agenda with hacking's less enlightened tendencies, while also acknowledging where hacking has shaped hacktivism. This chapter foregrounds in detail the more obsessive, addictive and pseudo-sexual aspects of the hacker mentality in order to provide a fuller context for the qualitatively new, distinguishing features of hacktivism.

It is often remarked that there are few women in hacking. There are very few accounts of female hackers and very little evidence that women have engaged in hacking (Jordan and Taylor 1998; Taylor 1999). Moreover, there are reasonably frequent accounts of online harassment and occasionally epic encounters with misogynist hackers (Gilboa 1996). While it would be misleading to brand all hackers sexist, there is no denying the competitive, masculine nature of the hacking community. In previous work we noted that misogyny was one of the six structuring internal principles of the hacking community (Jordan and Taylor 1998). From the perspective of gender, attempts to identify hackers as a radical resistance, and the connection of hacktivism to the anti-globalisation movement, may seem to be rather hollow claims.

As we will explore, the dominance of the end-in-itself mentality within hacking is arguably the single most important factor that has tended to exclude women. This point also suggests that if hacktivism contests the end-in-itself mentality then some reordering of gender within hacking may occur, and perhaps from this we can infer some reordering more generally within digital cultures.

This chapter also asks why the hack conveys a feeling of power that particularly appeals to young men, and further explores how such feelings of power are projected into rhetorical constructions, such as the comparison of cyberspace with the frontier land of the Wild West. This pioneer mentality is examined with reference to the political culture of technolibertarianism which is then contrasted with hacktivism's rise as a new form of technologically fuelled political activism. All through the accounts of hacking we are able to see a masculine conception of human relations running within these conceptions of power and control. On the basis of this discussion, it is possible to consider whether hacktivism offers a change. It can be argued that the early core values of hacking and its purported role as a site for cultural resistance and as a resource for stocks of countercultural practice were seriously undermined by the excesses of the computer underground and technolibertarian groups. In part hacktivism may well be crucial in reinventing the hacking ethos by revising its masculine bias. In an ironic twist, a culture initially deeply inimical to female participants may now rely upon them for its future development.

Hackers

> Wherever computer centres have become established . . . bright young men of dishevelled appearance, often with sunken glowing eyes, can be seen sitting at computer consoles, their arms tensed, and waiting to fire, their fingers, already poised to strike at the buttons and keys on which their attention seems to be as riveted as a gambler's on the rolling dice. When not so transfixed they often sit at tables strewn with computer print-outs over which they pore like possessed students of a cabalistic text. . . .They exist, at least when so engaged, only through and for the computers. These are computer bums, compulsive programmers. They are an international phenomenon.
>
> (Weizenbaum 1976: 125)

Weizenbaum's is the 'seminal' description of the archetypal male hacker distanced from the rest of mainstream society through the all-consuming nature of his high-tech pursuits. In an earlier description of the hacking community we undermined the pathologisation of hackers that so often follows such descriptions, yet we also noted the centrality of technical mastery to the hack (Jordan and Taylor 1998). It is the centrality of mastery that connects hacking, in its fundamentals, to what are perceived to be regressively masculine notions of competition, mastery and dominance. Within hacking, technical knowledge of both the artefact and its wider system are closely associated, and risk becoming ends in themselves. Therefore, appreciation of efficient technological systems frequently displaces social and political concerns about the effects and nature of systems with an overweening desire for the mastery of systems. This desire for mastery and obsession with technology cuts off concerns with wider politics and tends to restrict hacking's gaze to the narrowly technological.

In contrast, hacktivism, while staying faithful to the notion of the ingenuity of 'the hack', uses that ingenuity not as an end in itself but rather as the means to more outward-looking political ends. Mass action hacktivists seek to hack up tools to support a range of causes, such as the Zapatistas, while digitally correct hacktivists drive into the foreground the politics of information and the necessity of free information for free, egalitarian societies. This politicisation of hacking is complicated by the distinction between *mass action hacktivism* and the *digitally correct*. The former tends to draw heavily from broader social movements, in particular the anti-globalisation movement, and in doing so it draws in deeply felt concerns about equitable forms of organisation and political ends. Mass action hacktivists draw from their broader political frame of reference an alternative to the competitive mystique of hacking. Digitally correct hacktivism shares with mass action the sense of broader political ends. Digitally correct hacktivism both engages with grand issues of politics, for example with the rights of nation-states over their citizens, and brings those politics back to the hacking community. As one member of CDC cried to an audience of hackers at the hacktivist launch of Back Orifice: 'make it a little bit relevant'. However, the political end for the digitally correct remains an informational politics of ensuring efficient systems that enable free secure flows of information in cyberspace. Such a politics faces the problem of constantly falling back into a politics that excludes social, cultural and economic questions in favour of a concern for efficient systems; the operational at the expense of the substantive. As we will see, digitally correct hacktivism wavers between an outward-looking politics and the hacker obsession with equating technological means with social ends.

Male conformism

At twenty, he is still at the stage of a Boy Scout working on complicated knots just to please his parents. This type is held in high esteem in radio matters. He patiently builds sets whose most important parts he must buy ready-made, and scans the air for shortwave secrets, though there are none. As a reader of Indian stories and travel books, he once discovered unknown lands and cleared his path through the forest primeval. As radio ham, he becomes the discoverer of just those industrial products which are interested in being discovered by him. He brings nothing home that would not be delivered to his house.

(Adorno 1991 (1938): 54)

Adorno's description of the archetypal radio ham encapsulates not only the obsessive element of the hacker mentality but suggests its inherent political conservatism. In language redolent of Marx's notion that under capitalism commodities take on social relations while people increasingly begin to act as objects, we can follow Adorno and suggest that the hacker's gift for exploration is limited to 'those industrial products' that come to his attention. The limits of his explorations are predetermined by his *a priori* conformity to the demands of informational societies so that nothing is brought home that does not already fit within its framework. This notion of hackers as embodiments of the instrumental reason (which we previously saw Lash identify in Chapter 2 in terms of the 'shiny' network) is evident even in relatively sympathetic accounts of hacker culture. In relation to 'the hack' there is plenty of evidence that much hacker enjoyment stems from absorption within the self-enclosed systemic nature of technical artefacts and assemblages whether they be model railways or computers (Levy 1984; Lash 2002).

Such absorption with technical means, leaves little room for more outward-looking social concerns. Even the biggest non-technical concern of the early hacker generations tended to centre upon the issue of maximum access to computers. A key motivating force of the second generation of hackers, the hardware hackers who were instrumental in developing the first personal computers, was their relatively radical desire to democratise computing by bringing it to the people. However, they left in place an essential political problem over what happens when the issue of access to a technology dominates more substantive questions about the subsequent purposes of that access. For Baudrillard, this strategy is inherently flawed because, like Adorno's ham radio operator,

this 'revolution' at bottom conserves the category of transmitter, which it is content to generalize as separated, transforming everyone into his own transmitter, it fails to place the mass media system in check. We know the results of such phenomena as mass ownership of walkie-talkies, or everyone making their own cinema: a kind of personalized amateurism, the equivalent of Sunday tinkering on the periphery of the system.

(Baudrillard 1981: 182)

It is this limited concentration upon access rather than the ultimate purpose of that access that led to the early countercultural status of both Apple Computers and the hacker mentality that succumbed to corporate blandishments. Ironically, the former became the large corporation it had originally sought to undermine and the latter was co-opted for the commercial purposes of Microsoft and other corporations. In addition to concern over the inherent conservatism of 'Sunday tinkering on the periphery', there is also reason to question those forms of hacking that seek to engage with the system itself.

Hacking systems: the hands-on imperative

Wandering around the labyrinth of laboratories and storerooms, searching for the secrets of telephone switching in machine rooms, tracing paths of wires or relays in subterranean steam tunnels . . . for some it was common behavior, and there was no need to justify the impulse, when confronted with a closed door with an unbearably intriguing noise behind it, to open the door uninvited. And then, if there was no one to physically bar access to whatever was making that intriguing noise, to touch the machine, start flicking switches and noting responses, and eventually to loosen a screw, unhook a template, jiggle some diodes and tweak a few connections . . . things had meaning only if you found out how they worked. And how would you go about that if not by getting your hands on them?

(Levy 1984: 17)

Levy's description of early hacking culture highlights a particular form of hands-on curiosity as its key, determining feature. Hacking's innate intellectual brand of explorative curiosity ultimately constitutes a craving to understand *systems*. For the 'true hacker', the abstract quality of complexity is of more importance than the specific physical qualities of a particular technological artefact. At the same time, however, such curiosity cannot remain isolated on an abstract intellectual plane, it is inextricably linked to more mundane physical matters, such as the need for access to some form of embodied technology with the subsequent opportunity to exercise the *hands-on imperative*.

Hackers' brushes with the criminal system have led to vivid illustrations of the ubiquitous nature of their activity and the extent to which it consists of an ability to adapt to the circumstances. There is, for example, Kevin Poulsen's account of his time in prison: ' "I've learned a lot from my new neighbors," Poulsen, the quintessential cyberpunk . . . who describes hacking as performance art, said from behind the glass of the maximum security visitor's window. "Now I know how to light a cigarette from an outlet and how to make methamphetamine from chicken stock" ' (Fine 1995). The phone network was the archetypal system for the early precursors of hackers, the phone-phreaks, then the Internet provided the next complex technical system ripe for exploration. In addition to such examples of hands-on hacking, which involve ingenious manipulations of whatever artefacts are at hand, hacking can also refer more abstractly to the 'system' one is confronted with. A US hacker using the sobriquet Agent Steal, for example, published an article from federal prison entitled: 'Everything A Hacker Needs To Know About getting Busted By The Feds', the theme of which centres around the notion that the legal system, like any other system, is there to be hacked:

> The criminal justice system is a game to be played, both by prosecution and defense. And if you have to be a player, you would be wise to learn the rules of engagement. The writer and contributors of this file have learned the hard way. As a result we turned our hacking skills during the times of our incarceration towards the study of criminal law and, ultimately, survival. Having filed our own motions, written our own briefs and endured life in prison, we now pass this knowledge back to the hacker community. Learn from our experiences . . . and our mistakes.
>
> (Petersen 1997: 4)

This combination of interest in both abstract complexity and the physical manifestations of such complexity in all its forms, illustrates a key element of the hacking ethos that hacktivism and its interest in the capitalist system has sought to revive. Before the rise of hacktivism, an important element of the original hacker ethos had increasingly tended to be lost in the minutiae and excessively close identification with the most important hacker artefact to date: the computer.

For hackers, hacktivism is a moment of confrontation with their assumed politics. It is an irruption into the collective imagination of hackers when hacktivists begin to demand and question why hacks occur or to engage in extended politicised discussions of why they are conducting hacktivist hacks. Various assumptions made by hackers – such as the moment of masterful, illicit and simple intervention into a technology is a good thing in and of itself – are questioned by hacktivism. This is an ambivalent process. As we have seen, some mass action hacktivists are willing to confront hacking to the extent of misrepresenting its motivations. For example, we have seen Dominguez and Wray from EDT reinterpret the demand for bandwidth or digital rights from hackers as a demand for rights for inanimate objects. At the same time, mass action hacktivists and digitally correct hacktivists put their fingers firmly on an uncomfortable point in hacking: Why do it? Why make hacks and how do you defend whatever good or bad comes from them?

Informational intimacy: cyberpunks meet microserfs

> He closed his eyes. . . . It came on again, gradually, a flickering, nonlinear flood of fact and sensory data, a kind of narrative conveyed in surreal jumpcuts and juxtapositions. It was vaguely like riding a rollercoaster that phased in and out of existence at random, impossibly rapid intervals, changing altitude, attack, and direction with each pulse of nothingness, except that the shifts had nothing to do with any physical orientation, but rather with lightning alternations in paradigm and symbol system. The data had never been intended for human input.
>
> (Gibson 1986: 40).

> Further personality fragmentation and a breakdown of empathy lead to 'cyberpsychosis'. Behind this idea lies a long history of anxieties about 'dehumanization' by technology; a quintessentially humanist point of view which sees technology as an autonomous, runaway force that has come to displace the natural right of individuals to control themselves and their environment.
>
> (Ross 1991: 160)

Cyberpunk fiction, as illustrated in the above quotation from Gibson's agenda-setting novel *Neuromancer*, portrays with exaggerated clarity the above-average intensity, intimacy and enjoyment derived by hackers from their interactions with technology. The fact that the fictional portrayal contains an instructive kernel of truth is indicated by the way in which Levy's factual account of hacking underlines cyberpunk's depiction of the human/machine symbiosis and emphasises the extreme ideal of identification with information systems that the early hackers were striving to achieve. He observed that, 'Real optimum programming, of course, could only be accomplished when every obstacle between you and the pure computer was eliminated – an ideal that probably won't be fulfilled until hackers are somehow biologically merged with computers' (Levy 1984: 126). He described how, to some extent at least, the earliest hackers achieved this feeling by attaining, 'a state of pure concentration. . . . When you had all that information glued to your cerebral being, it was almost as if your mind had merged into the environment of the computer' (Levy 1984: 37). Jacques Vallee similarly described such a process in relation to a hacker called Chip Tango: 'He never speaks of "using a machine" or "running a program". He leaves those expressions to those engineers of the old school. Instead, he will say that he "attaches his consciousness" to a particular process. He butterflies his way across the net, picking up a link here, an open socket there' (Vallee 1984: 136).

Such comfort, to the point of melding, with complex forms of technology contrasts with the more generally held societal fears of viral times. Yet despite the fact that cyberpunks clearly represent a highly modernised and implicitly praised form of the maverick spirit of the Western cowboy, cyberpunk is also riddled with examples of the negative consequences of their intimate relationship with technology. The anomie encountered by the detective genre's Private Eye as he plies his deductive trade in the anonymous city is transformed for the console cowboy into both the lawless immateriality of the matrix he mentally navigates and the feral physicality of the post-urban dystopia he struggles to survive within. The cerebral freedom afforded by the matrix is often enjoyed at a physical price within the real world. This is the case with our first glimpses of the hacker Neo in the film *The Matrix*. He is an alienated, unhealthy individual confined physically to a small room while he navigates cyberspace. Similarly, the film's freedom fighters are physically confined to a small, rusting, threatened spacecraft from which they roam immaterial lands, imbued with superhuman powers.

While individual explorations of the capitalist matrix produce a personal buzz, cyberpunk's social settings are invariably presented in dire, dystopian terms with physical violence as a constant background threat. The willingness and ability of cyberpunks/hackers to enjoy informational intimacy sets them apart. When Neo in the Matrix first has high level skills uploaded into his brain, suddenly teaching him advanced fighting techniques, his face registers severe shock and he simply barks out the word 'More'. Affinity with, and control of, information, however, may be mutually exclusive due to the seductively invasive qualities of cyberspace; its losing-of-oneself quality that paradoxically (given its essentially abstract nature) has been imbued in both cyberpunk and hacker accounts with a sexual frisson.

> he'd cry for it, cry in his sleep, and wake alone in the dark, curled in his capsule in some coffin hotel, his hands clawed into the bedslab, temperfoam bunched between his fingers, trying to reach the console that wasn't there. . . . For Case, who lived for the bodiless exultation of cyberspace, it was the Fall. In the bars he'd frequented as a cowboy hotshot, the elite stance involved a certain relaxed contempt for the flesh. The body was meat. Case fell into the prison of his own flesh.
>
> (Gibson 1984: 11, 12)

Despite this language of physicality, such enjoyment contains an essential contradiction since it is premised upon a sense of 'bodiless exultation'. The pseudo-sexual pleasure of informational intimacy may be enjoyed, paradoxically, only at the price of a loss of contact with the physical environment. Although the disjuncture between the physical and the abstract receives its most dramatic expression in the dehumanising concerns of science-fiction cyberpunk, it is also a strong element of Coupland's socially realistic *Microserfs* in which a lack of comfort with one's body is a recurrent theme.

> I don't even do any sports anymore and my relationship with my body has gone all weird. I used to play soccer three times a week and now I feel like a boss in charge of an underachiever. I feel like my body is a station wagon in which I drive my brain around, like a suburban mother taking the kids to hockey practice.
>
> (Coupland 1995: 4)

Such examples match closely with descriptions of how hackers typically pay little attention to their bodily needs or physical appearance while absorbed by their activity (Hafner and Lyon 1996; Freedman and Mann 1997). This lack of interest in bodily matters periodically and perversely culminated in an annual competition run by the hacker community at MIT to find the ugliest geek on campus (Levy 1984). Even where hackers present themselves as physically adept individuals, their physical activity is more often than not presented as an alternative to or escape from their lives as a hacker. For example, Tstutomu Shimomura's account of his detective-like cyber-chase of the famed hacker Kevin Mitnick, intersperses the abstraction of his computer programming with trips to snowy mountains to gain a skiing instructor's qualification (Shimomura 1995). The profound effect of this decreasing importance of the physical and, as we discussed in Chapter 2, the concomitant rise of the abstract is recognised by Ullman as an integral aspect of the world of non-fictional computer programmers, whose information-dense lives necessitate embracing the sterile mindset of a microserf:

> We give ourselves over to the sheer fun of the technical, to the nearly sexual pleasure of the clicking thought-stream. Some part of me mourns, but I know there is no other way: human needs must cross the line into code. They must pass through this semiperme-able membrane where urgency, fear, and hope are filtered out, and only reason travels across. . . . Actual human confusions cannot live here. Everything we want accomplished, everything the system is to provide, must be denatured in its crossing to the machine, or else the system will die.
>
> (Ullman 1997: 15)

Another explanatory comparison made in cyberpunk fiction to convey the intensity of immersive informational experiences is that of the drug-induced psychedelic trip. Accessing information is like: 'falling into bliss and numbers . . . numbers and bliss . . . the numbers overriding the bliss so that the whole world seemed like a mathematical formula . . . full of a slow ecstasy it was, a long, drawn-out parade of tenderness' (Noon 1995: 224). Despite their dramatic nature, the relevance of such fictional portrayals to the non-fictional world of computing should not be underestimated. Ullman, writing as a female programmer, uses similar terms to describe the state of mind among her male colleagues:

> The world as humans understand it and the world as it must be explained to computers come together in the programmer in a strange state of disjunction. The project begins in the programmer's mind with the beauty of a crystal. I remember the feel of a system

at the early stages of programming, when the knowledge I am to represent in code seems lovely in its structuredness. For a time, the world is a calm, mathematical place. Human and machine seem attuned to a cut-diamond-like state of grace. Once in my life I tried methamphetamine: that speed high is the only state that approximates the feel of a project at its inception. Yes, I understand. Yes, it can be done. Yes, how straightforward. Oh, yes. I see.

(Ullman 1997: 21)

This ambivalent tone represents a key aspect of the roots of real-world hacking's lack of radicality to which hacktivism is partly responding. A major feature of the ambivalence of both cyberpunks and their real-world hacker counterparts is the way in which their technical mastery is often gained at the price of an excessively invasive and ultimately lonely intimacy with informational environments. The positive cerebral buzz they enjoy from engagement with abstract systems is at the expense of real-world groundedness. Ullmann's account provides a vivid sense of the hacker mentality's profound need to view the world in coded terms. Although, at times, we have seen this need described as a form of sublimated sexuality, the repeated desire to enter and then be at one with the impersonal system can perhaps best be understood in terms normally reserved for discussions of addiction.

Informational addiction

The hacker wants to break in. Breaking in is the addictive principle of hacking. . . . It produces anxiety, as it is a melancholic exercise in endless loss. . . . The experience of the limit that cyberspace affords is an anxious, addictive experience in which the real appears as withdrawal and loss. . . . The matrix is too complex and fragmented to offer itself to any one unifying gaze. . . . Hence, the attraction of the cyberspace addiction: to jack in is briefly, thrillingly, to get next to the power; not to be able to jack in is impotence. Moreover, the cyberspace addiction, the hacker mystique, posits power through anonymity. . . . It is a dream of recovering power and wholeness by seeing wonders and by not being seen. But what a strange and tangled dream, this power that is only gained through matching your synapses to the computer's logic, through beating the system by being the system.

(Moreiras 1993: 197–8)

The image of flesh as a prison and the real as loss are particularly forceful expressions of the uneasy sense of the physical that the hacker relationship to abstraction promotes. For hackers a similar, if less marked, affinity is shown for 'the system' whether it comes in the form of complex phone or computer networks: ' "There's a real love–hate relationship between us and the phone company. We don't particularly appreciate the bureaucracy that runs it, but we love the network itself," he says, lingering the world love. "The network is the greatest thing to come along in the world" ' (Colligan 1982). The obsessive body-neglecting qualities of cyberpunk's fictional depiction of what is involved by mentally 'jacking into' the matrix of information is similar to the imagery of addiction used by real-life hackers. Hacker Maelstrom claimed:

> I just do it because it makes me feel good, as in better than anything else that I've ever experienced. Computers are the only thing that have ever given me this feeling . . . the adrenaline rush I get when I'm trying to evade authority, the thrill I get from having written a program that does something that was supposed to be impossible to do, and the ability to have social relations with other hackers are all very addictive. I get depressed when I'm away from a networked computer for too long. I find conversations held in cyberspace much more meaningful and enjoyable than conversing with people in physical-reality real mode. . . . I consider myself addicted to hacking. If I were ever in a position where I knew my computer activity was over for the rest of my life, I would suffer withdrawal.
> (cited in Taylor 1999: 107)

> rushing through the phone line like heroin through an addicts veins, an electronic pulse is sent out, a refuge from the day-to-day incompetencies is sought . . . a board is found. 'This is it . . . this is where I belong.'
> (The Mentor 1986)

The major reason for the 'relaxed contempt for the flesh' exhibited by cyberpunk characters is their addictive affinity with the rich data environment sometimes called the matrix. While the Latin root of this phrase (*mater*) offers rich opportunities for womb-related and psychoanalytically inspired theorising, there remains the very practical issue of the obvious gender disparity of those who work most closely within its technical framework.

The matrix: no place for a woman?

Having explored certain aspects of the hacking mentality that make it prone to interpreting technologies as asocial things whose manipulation is a hacker's path to a bodiless salvation, we can now turn to some of the consequences of this stance. Although we have touched on hacktivism as we have worked through this chapter, we are mainly drawing conclusions about hacking in order to see this influence on hacktivism at work. We will now look at gender as a key factor in the irruption of hacktivism into hacking.

As with all discussions of gender, it is important to note at the outset that it is neither biologically given nor is it a simple, mutually exclusive social and cultural division. It is all too easy when discussing gender to slip into stereotypes that pander to existing cultural preconceptions but bear little relation to the socially and culturally constructed complexities of gender in the twenty-first century. We do not have space here to detail such debates but heedful of this danger of over-stereotyped interpretations of what is masculine and what feminism we seek to qualify their meanings as they arise.

> A new study by the US Department of Commerce reports that only 9 per cent of engineers, 26.9 per cent of systems analysts and computer scientists, and 28.5 per cent of computer programmers are women. In 1984, 37 per cent of computer science degrees went to women; by 1998 that number was 16 per cent. . . . And studies show that women working in IT now make 72 cents on the dollar when compared to their male counterparts. In the mainstream, above-ground, work-a-day world of high technology, women are becoming less visible rather than more so. Little wonder that they're downright invisible in the élite band of digital cowboys who call themselves hackers. . . . Girl hackers are as rare as Linux code in a Windows factory.
>
> (Lynch 2000)

> Women often feel about as welcome as a system crash.
>
> (Miller 1995: 49)

The above quotations illustrate the extent of hacking's gender bias. The reason for this disproportionate absence of women relates to the social conditions of hacking and computing in general. These have made it less likely for women to be involved in programming activities in the first place and have created a hostile environment for women if they do choose to get involved. The combination of hacking's esoteric and high-tech knowledge seems to provide a heady mix that produces manifestations of aggression in the form of pointless acts of destruction and sexist behaviour:

> Jane Del Favero, the network security manager at New York University, has read the riot act to plenty of students caught for breaking into machines. Not one of them has been female. 'I'm not sure if there is much about hacking that attracts the average teenage girl. My impression is that they're not interested in the pointless glory of defacing a web site', she said.
>
> (Segan 2000a)

Many 'true' hackers would claim that pointless vandalism within computing is the work of criminally motivated crackers not hackers. However, as we have seen in Chapter 1, crackers remain a component of the sprawling hacker community. It also remains true that even when such vandalism involves at least an element of technological ingenuity, it seldom seems to be an activity that appeals to female programmers. It appears that women, or the feminine, are much less likely to respect technological ingenuity for its own sake and are much more concerned with the ultimate ends to which such ingenuity is to be applied.

> The female hackers say they're interested in technology for what it is or what it does, not so they can break it and watch people suffer. RosieX, editor of the Australian feminist technology magazine *GeekGirl*, said cybervandalism was a 'masturbatory' activity she'd prefer to leave to the boys. 'I really abhor most of the crimes. I find them petulant and, yes, more male than female. I find nothing clever about dismantling an individual's system', she said.
>
> (Segan 2000a)

In addition to the barriers to female involvement created by gratuitously destructive acts, there is a general level of sexism ranging from the extreme to the mild: 'The experience of women at the entry levels of the hacking scene, mostly in online chat groups, is one of relentless sexual harassment. It is a hard battle for women to be respected in a culture dominated by teenage boys' (Segan 2000b).

Turkle provides the suitably suggestive categories of 'hard' and 'soft' mastery to account for the disproportionate presence of men within hacking; hacking's aggressive nature reflects men's predisposition towards 'hard mastery' whereas its lack of female participants reflects their preference for 'soft mastery'. For Turkle, hard mastery 'is the imposition of will over the machine through the implementation of a plan. . . . Soft mastery is more interactive . . . try this, wait for a response, try something else, let the overall shape emerge from interaction with the medium. It is more like a conversation than a monologue' (Turkle 1984: 102–3). Turkle's two pyschological categories for use within computing, while reflecting stark differences in the approaches of the genders, avoids resorting to biological determinism by retaining a sense of the situation's socially constructed nature:

> In our culture girls are taught the characteristics of soft mastery – negotiation, compromise, give-and-take – as psychological virtues, while models of male behaviour stress decisiveness and the imposition of will. . . . Scientific objects are placed in a 'space' psychologically far away from the world of everyday life, from the world of emotions and relationships. Men seem able, willing and invested in constructing these separate 'objective' worlds, which they can visit as neutral observers. . . . We can see why women might experience a conflict between this construction of science and what feels like 'their way' of dealing with the world, a way that leaves more room for continuous relationships between the self and other.
>
> (Turkle 1984: 107, 115)

This revelling within abstractions and the close engagement with a technology that is conceived of as both end and means, underpins a regressive masculinity that we argue has dominated hacking. We use the term regressive to indicate a masculinity that takes on, for much of the time, an exaggerated concern to define itself through competition, mastery and domination. It is over both machines and other humans that hackers seek domination but it is always through technologies that domination is established. If we recall the example of the DDOS attacks mounted by Wicked against Steve Gibson's website (pp. 74–7), we see an example of this need for domination through technologies. Gibson's crime for Wicked was of having been reported by some other hackers as having used the term 'script-kiddies'. This utterly flimsy pretext for the devastating attack launched by Wicked's zombies is an example of someone with a need for domination through the demonstration of their skills seeking a reason, any reason, to launch an assault.

There is of course no reason why women could not launch such attacks. Our point is that any women doing so would be engaging their subjectivity with a regressive masculinity. Similarly, there are examples of males who do not fully take on the competitive, dominating masculinity we have seen in hacking. The point remains that the obsessive engagement with technology as both means and end, that is accompanied by a related desire to lose the body, supports and is engaged with a particular form of masculinity that runs through hacking. In the remainder of this chapter we will concentrate on the proclivity of hacker culture to revel in artificially abstract constructions, before our analysis in Chapter 7 of hacktivism's diametrically opposed desire to use technology only in so far as it can contribute to a renewed emphasis on politics.

Cyberspace as the Wild West

> Hackers are . . . the kind of restless, impatient, sometimes amoral or egocentric spirit that chafes at any kind of restriction or boundary, the kind of spirit (either 'free' or 'outlaw', depending on how you look at it) that bristles resentfully at other people's laws, rules, regulations, and expectations, and relentlessly seeks a way to get over or under or around those rules. . . . In other words, very much the same sort of spirit that drove the people, who, for good and ill, opened up the American West, the kind of spirit that produced far-sighted explorers as well as cattle rustlers and horse thieves, brave pioneers as well as scurvy outlaw gangs, and that built the bright new cities of the Plains at the cost of countless thousands of Native American lives.
>
> (Dann and Dozois 1996: xiii).

> We had this notion of ourselves as Butch Cassidy and the Sundance Kid. It was just going to be Mitch and John alone against the governments of the free world! But we felt so electronically amplified we felt we could probably do as well that way as any other.
>
> (John Perry Barlow cited in Jordan 1999b: 82)

Wild West imagery has permeated discussions of cybercultures. It has also served to encourage the projection of macho personalities by hackers. In the above quotation Barlow is referring to his and Mitch Kapor's work during the founding of one of the first ever civil liberties groups concerned solely with cyberspatial liberties. The name of this organisation is telling for our purpose: the Electronic *Frontier* Foundation. Frontier rather than the title many might expect from a civil liberties organisation, the Electronic *Freedom* Foundation. Barlow notes of many in cyberspace: 'the actual natives are solitary and independent, sometimes to the point of sociopathy. It is of course a perfect breeding ground for outlaws and new ideas about liberty' (Barlow 1990: 45). Laura Miller identifies the implicitly masculine and sexual aspect of the frontier metaphor as crucial for developing an understanding of the gendered basis of cyberspace:

> The classic Western narrative is . . . concerned with social relationships. . . . In these stories, the frontier is a lawless society of men, a milieu in which physical strength, courage, and personal charisma supplant institutional authority and violent conflict is the accepted means of settling disputes. The Western narrative connects pleasurably with the American romance of individualistic masculinity; small wonder that the predominantly male founders of the Net's culture found it so appealing. When civilisation arrives on the frontier, it comes dressed in skirts and short pants.
>
> (Miller 1995: 52)

The Wild West is a founding myth of cyberspace. The metaphor has been an important ideological influence upon the conceptualisation of this inherently immaterial land. It has allowed individuals to conceive themselves in relation to cyberspace in order to grasp and use a space that transgresses so many familiar, physically based intuitions about how to live in the world. In this sense, 'The fundamental power of the metaphor of the frontier is to take as protean a form of communication as cyberspace and conceive it as space' (Jordan 1999a: 176). Once conceived as a frontier space, cyberspace is open to colonisation. Miller draws our attention to the ways this metaphoric imposition of frontiers, cowboys and, less visibly, colonisation, embeds certain masculine and exploitative social relations into early conceptions of cyberspace's nature (Jordan 1999: 172–6).

Miller uses the phrase 'skirts and short pants' in order to capture the dismissive attitude the male self-styled pioneers of cyberspace have to those who would seek to regulate their domain. Despite being fuelled by such rhetorically rebellious independence, it should be clear from our previous account of how the initially countercultural qualities of hacking were co-opted into a more commercially friendly form of computer programming, that such independence still requires the institution of the market. However, the most vocal and powerful expression of the implicitly masculine anti-regulation approach to computing is the world view that can be loosely described by the term technolibertarianism and to which we now turn.

Technolibertarianism

> the most virulent form of philosophical technolibertarianism is a kind of scary, psychologically brittle, prepolitical autism. It bespeaks a lack of human connection and a discomfort with the core of what many of us consider it means to be human. It's an inability to reconcile the demands of being individual with the demands of participating in society, which coincides beautifully with a preference for, and glorification of, being the solo commander of one's computer in lieu of any other economically viable behavior. Computers are so much more rule-based, controllable, fixable, and comprehensible than any human will ever be. As many political schools of thought do, these technolibertarians make a philosophy out of a personality defect.
>
> (Boorsook 2000: 15)

The term *technolibertarian* refers to those closely involved within the computer industry who espouse strong libertarian and free-market political principles and closely associate them with the promotion of the e-economy. Their views frequently articulate a preference for a society as free as possible from regulation, social ties and, generally, the obligations that inevitably stem from community relations in the real world. John Gilmore a hacker (in the original sense of the word) put his commitment to libertarianism this way:

> I think part of the reason that the Internet is more libertarian is just because they've winnowed out a lot of the other stuff; they look at

socialism and say 'well how come you people are still living in hovels?' They look at authoritarian societies and say 'well how come you don't get the great breakthroughs and how come you don't get the rapid diffusion of ideas through society? How come things just don't evolve as quickly there?' The answers lie in the philosophical roots of society; you'll do what you're told not what you think you'll be best at, not what will make you happy and people tend to be a lot more effective and a lot more imaginative when they're doing what they've chosen to do. When there are few barriers to them doing that – you don't need a government licence for that, you don't need to wait six months for permission to do that, you don't need to check with anyone!

(Gilmore 1996)

Technolibertarians take ideas such as Gilmore's and use them to reach a kind of end-point, a logical and extreme extension of the hacker beliefs we have so far been exploring. As such, their views should be seen not so much as what hackers think, but rather, as a crystallisation of some of the most masculinised tendencies within hacking.

This, of course, also makes technolibertarians a good, clear illustration of not only the hard mastery tendencies we have previously identified but also the type of mindset that is perfectly suited for close identification with the abstract systems of advanced informational capitalism. In technolibertarianism, the social gaucheness associated with the geeky image of hackers is transformed into a political philosophy that spares little time for communitarian social values. To compensate for such alienation, technolibertarianism promotes a preference for the predictability and abstract purity of programming which: 'in a way pays weird homage to a Freudian view of the world – all base emotion and power drives and secret motivations – where higher brain functions such as altruism or empathy or trying to do what's right or mixed emotions are left out of the mix' (Boorsook 2000: 92). In what could be termed a form of 'digital Darwinism', technolibertarianism merges the abstract, binary codes of cyberspace with: 'a view of human nature that reduces everything to the contractual, to economic rational decision-making, which ignores the larger social mesh that makes living as primates in groups at least somewhat bearable, when the weight of days becomes intolerable' (Boorsook 2000: 110).

The rhetorical excesses of pioneering and technolibertarian language provide linguistic cover for an apparent unwillingness to deal with real-world uncertainties while simultaneously providing an expression of virility for an otherwise defensive nerdy culture. Confidence in the ultimate 'programmability' of the real world can be applied even to one's personal relationships. For example, Boorsook uses the term 'Nerverts' to describe a subculture within technolibertarianism characterised by the conflation of extreme or unusual sexualities and the belief that the model of computer programming can be effectively applied even to such intimate personal relations. Nerverts replace the potential confusions and vagueness of amorous cues and seductive interplay with a preference for much more obviously structured forms of interaction. From a perspective where 'monogamy is viewed as emotional terrorism' (Boorsook 2000: 100), such activities as role playing and consensual S&M, create a much more predictable and straightforwardly coded emotional environment.

The application of an informational approach even to intimate relations is reflected in the words of Robin Roberts, the founder of the nervert S&M Backdrop Club: 'the elaborate negotiations of S-M courtship are like network protocols . . . and handshaking [a system for two different pieces of hardware to establish communications connections]' (Boorsook 2000: 105). The fact that Roberts also teaches classes on how to read another person's body language for programmers within Silicon Valley leads Boorsook to make the acerbic comment that: 'Using their brains to construct and act out a fantasy, reducing that most maddening and paradoxical and mysterious of human activities, sex and attraction, to codes – it's a magnificent case of making lemonade out of overcerebrated lemons' (Boorsook 2000: 105). These and the previous examples of excessive identification with code serve to indicate some of the consistent barriers that have existed across the first five generations of hackers. Engagement with messy contingency is passed over in favour of abstract, more predictable systems. Having ventured to the extremes of technolibertarianism, we can conclude this line of argument by looking at the non-pejorative concept of the hacker as a parasite in order to clearly contrast the essential differences between hacking and hacktivism.

The hacker as parasite

Parasitism constitutes an eccentric operation that exceeds the traditional logic of either/or or what is sometimes called the 'law of noncontradiction'. The parasite occupies a structurally unique position that is neither simply inside nor simply outside. It is the outside in the inside and the inside outside itself.

(Gunkel 2001: 5)

Gunkel draws on Derrida to discuss hacking in terms of an essentially 'parasitic activity' in the sense that: 'It is an undertaking that always requires a host system in which and on which to operate' (Gunkel 2001: 5). The term is not used judgementally, but rather as a way of approaching the issue of the complex symbiotic relationship hackers have with the overarching system that provides them with their numerous minor systems. Gunkel's analysis provides an important context for debates over the significance of the decline in the potentially radical political qualities of the original hacker ethic witnessed by the advent of crackers and microserfs.

Hacking, for example, depends on the good health of its host for the necessary conditions for its own operations: 'as a parasite, hacking draws all its strength, strategies and tools from the system on which and in which it operates. The hack does not, strictly speaking, introduce anything new into the system on which it works but derives everything from the host's own protocols and procedures' (Gunkel 2001: 6). It is at this point that a slight tension arises in Gunkel's analysis because, despite hacking's reliance upon the structures and processes of the system it inhabits, he also maintains that: 'Hacking deliberately exceeds recuperative gestures that would put its activities to work for the continued success and development of the host's system' (Gunkel 2001: 7). 'True' hacking is in the system but not of the system and to remain true to itself it remains dependent upon, but not beholden to, that system. Such an analysis is in keeping with our previous account of the way in which the original hacker ethic was betrayed by subsequent generations of hackers. The 'pure' form of hacking capable of maintaining the rather delicate balance between reliance and independence is likely to be both short-lived and more like a goal than a steady communal state for hacking.

In contrast to 'pure parasitical' hacking, we have seen throughout this chapter how the closeness to the codes and protocols of their environment has in fact encouraged hackers to engage in ways that allow, if not promote, recuperation. In practice, independent, unadulterated parasitism has not been maintained and the hacker mentality has actively reinforced the capitalist system, especially once the excesses of technolibertarianism are reached. It is this slippage that accounts for the relative ease with which the 'pure' intellectual focus and countercultural edge to the first hacking groups became much more commercially minded as their technical activities created products suited to both computing and commodity codes.

Even when it does not succumb to corporate blandishments, hacking's parasitical nature creates problems for notions of radicality. Perhaps most obviously radicality is undermined by reliance upon a system one cannot fundamentally disrupt because it provides your essential field of action. This explains why despite their potential countercultural status as powerful disrupters, hackers who engage in destructive informational activities tended to be censured heavily from within hacker culture itself. Less surprisingly, censure also came from those within mainstream culture who sought to utilise such opprobrium for their own boundary-forming purposes (Taylor 1999). Thus Gunkel quotes Richard Stallman to point out that a direct attempt to use technical systems to oppose the overarching system is readily co-opted by those who make political gain from such social conflicts: 'By shaping ourselves into the enemy of the establishment, we uphold the establishment' (Gunkell 2001: 7). Within hacktivism and as we shall discuss in more detail in this book's conclusion, this critique points most powerfully at digitally correct hacktivists for whom information suits nearly any politics. Though we have seen it can also be applied to culture jammers. Such hacktivists can thus be accused of freeing information for any political purpose, however progressive or regressive.

In response to the potential dangers of getting too close to the system, Gunkell proposes an alternative interpretation of hacking's significance.

> it constitutes a blasphemous form of intervention that learns how to manipulate and exploit necessary lacunae that are constitutive of but generally unacknowledged by that which is investigated. Hacking does so not to be mischievous or clever, but to locate, demonstrate, and reprogram the systems of rationality that not only determine cyberspace but generally escape critical investigation precisely because they are taken for granted and assumed to be infallible.
>
> (Gunkel 2001: 20)

Gunkel's whole approach, as implied in the title of his book *Hacking Cyberspace*, is to see in hacking the basis for a fundamental reinterpretation and questioning of the dominant frameworks of the information revolution. Rather than hacking's ingenuity and technical cleverness being ends in themselves, they represent for Gunkel ongoing tools in a critical, questioning process. In the final sentence of his book's introduction he argues that the outcome of this process: 'is neither good or bad, positive or negative, nor constructive or destructive but constitutes a general strategy by which to explore and manipulate the systems of rationality' (Gunkel 2001: 21).

We have seen in previous sections that, in practice, the general strategies of hacking have suffered from adapting too closely to the systems of rationality they seek to manipulate. Implicit in our account has been the suggestion that the hacker mentality's inherent tendency to privilege systemic logic works strongly against the generation of a critical political sensitivity. The political radicality it has exhibited has tended towards the articulation and promotion of greater engage-ment with systemic logic through the alignment of laissez-faire and informational protocols. From a political perspective there is a marked gap in the use of hacking techniques for more counter-systemic activity and it is a gap that hacktivism has begun to fill.

Hacktivism: hacking the system

> Their motivations for producing technology oscillate between compulsion and ethical imperative. It is a type of addiction mania that carries its own peculiar contradictions. Since such production is extremely labor-intensive, requiring permanent focus, a special-ized fixation emerges that is beneficial within the immediate realm of techno-production, but is extremely questionable outside its spatial–temporal zone. The hacker is generally obsessed with efficiency and order. In producing decentralized technology, a fetish for the algorithmic is understandable and even laudable; however, when it approaches a totalizing aesthetic, it has the potential to become damaging to the point of complicity with the state.
>
> (CAE 1994: 137)

We previously cited Adorno on radio hams (see pp. 118–19) to suggest that part of the hacker mentality is indebted to the socio-economic status quo that provides it with its tools and systems. The above assessment from the Critical Art Ensemble neatly summarises the point we have reached in our argument that hackers' relationship to the system is all too easily co-opted into the recuperative actions Gunkel identified as fatally undermining to the 'true' hacker project. But hacktivism is a new form of political activism that seeks many things, one of which – strangely enough – is to return hacking to its original senses without falling into the complicit conformism described throughout this chapter. Since hacktivism has only risen to prominence since the late 1990s, it is too early to say whether it will be successful at mixing technological ingenuity with a more critical political perspective. The early signs, however, are strong in so far as it has already avoided much of the male-dominated aspects of computing we have outlined in this chapter. In some forms, hacktivism is much more inclusive and its roots in political and social activism offer considerable potential to close the gender gap and to reintroduce more real-world concerns to the 'means equals ends'-oriented constructions of male programming culture. We will consider this new potential before taking up cautionary notes sounded by some other trends in hacktivism.

In interview, the female hacktivist Carmin Karasic provided a positive account of the increasing contribution women are making to online political activity. It is interesting to note that her role within the EDT was predominantly on the technical side. She provides a useful embodiment of hacktivism's potential to apply a technical focus to overt political ends. Her design of the hacktivist tool FloodNet was premised upon a desire to encourage mass participation rather than the technical elegance required for the classic hack. This is one instantiation of mass action hacktivism's creation of impaired technologies for an unimpaired politics. The difference this marks between the hacker and hacktivist mentality was reflected in the angry response Karasic received from Dutch hackers and for whom the point of an online political protest remains subordinate to the larger importance of protecting the Internet:

> They have a notion of technical elegance above all else – they got annoyed that FloodNet just clogged up the Internet. This goes back to the pinging of servers, and issues like pinging the server on the way there rather than the channel on the way back. . . . Dutch hackers want focused and targeted attacks to avoid clogging up like that.
>
> (Karasic, email interview 2001)

As these inherently more political aspects of hacktivism focus much more closely on the relationship between the individual and his/her wider environment, it is perhaps unsurprising that the new activity provides a more inclusive environment than old-style hacking. Karasic suggests that hacktivism retains 'true hacking's' desire to master the system, but opens up its focus to go beyond the more limited technical concerns of hackers:

> Hacktivism isn't restricted to just hackers (conventionally defined) it is much more about bending the technology to suit your political cause and that's something that's not just interesting to men. Women are taking a bigger and bigger role and starting to be more influential. Women are much more about negotiation and consensus and as hacktivism involves more women, hacktivist tools are likely to involve more participation. The lone, male hacker tends to do things with their own little piece of code, but women are much less likely to do that, they're much more likely to develop code that does something for human causes. Hackers aren't so much interested in social issues, they're much more interested in the human/machine interaction like the kid who unpicks the clock, so they're much more interested in things rather than people.
>
> (Karasic, email interview 2001)

This is a clear enunciation of mass action's desires to engage a broad politics, most often informed by the anti-globalisation movement. It is here we find some potential power within hacktivism to redress the drift toward such macho extremes as technolibertarianism and to find places for a rebalancing of gender within hacking and cybercultures generally. If it is true, as it seems to be, that digital cultures often take a lead from the hacking community, then here we might be witnessing broader cybercultural shifts than just ones within hacking.

But the concerns for the Internet and its structures voiced to Karasic by some Dutch hackers reflect not only hacker concerns but also the concerns of the digitally correct. These hacktivists seek to make the Internet flow constantly and unrestrainedly. The taking down of websites through mass actions is anathema to digitally correct hacktivists in their often single-minded pursuit of the human rights to information. We can here see some of the internal complexity of hacktivism. The closer relationship of the digitally correct to hacking need not result in any disagreement with mass action hacktivists on issues of machismo or gender balances within hacking and cybercultures, but it would also be naive to expect the deep roots of hacking in an alienated and regressive masculinity to simply disappear. One quick example will suffice to suggest this is the case.

When Back Orifice 2000 was released it came complete, as all things in the twenty-first century must, with a logo. This was clearly the back view of someone of indeterminate gender, bending over, their anus prominently drawn as if it were a target. Given the use of Back Orifice 2000's role in penetrating systems, it is hard not to draw the sniggering conclusion that BO was here being advertised as a form of digital sodomy. The gesture back to hacking's locker room machismo, complete with the slightly hysterical fear of sodomy that is on display (given that illicit penetration of one's computer system is something generally to fear), provides one graphic connection to hacking's, and by extension potentially hacktivism's, integration of a regressive masculinity.

At the same time we must refuse the simplicity of a picture in which mass action hacktivism is 'good' and digitally correct hacktivism 'bad'. After all, the digitally correct focus on maintaining an Internet that will allow mass actions to proceed. Further, the rights to information that the digitally correct uphold are also human rights, which, given the importance of information to twenty-first-century societies, may be considered fundamental. Finally, we should recognise that it is mainly from digitally correct hacktivists, who unlike mass action hacktivists do attend hacker conventions and are adopted with pride by many hackers, that the hacking community is being reinvented, in part, as a politicised community. While mass action hacktivists might seem the more politically savoury to many outside virtuality, within the immaterial realms of hackers it is the digitally correct who are using their deep concern with human rights to information to communicate to hackers just how political their techno-obsessions really are. It is the digitally correct who may be teaching hackers more about politics than mass action hacktivists, because the digitally correct may be re-politicising the very ends and means of hacking – the technological system.

But now we have passed beyond hacking and reached hacktivism. In the next chapter we will explore hacktivism's political manifesto that results from this preference for people over things.

Conclusion

Hackerdom with all its failings and foibles, eccentricities and extremism is just a techno-nerd boys' club. Its membership is male not because men's biological urges drive them to sit in front of a computer screen and wangle their way through firewalls. Its membership is male because women don't possess the technological savvy and depth that are the price of admission. . . . Call it a testosterone problem. Call it a technology problem. Call it an economic, social, political, it's-those-darned-whining-feminists-again problem. But while we're pontificating and proselytizing about hacker danger and its threat to our national security and American way of life, let's also remember that those hackers are bound to be boys. Sophomoric, solipsistic, and scruffy. Technologically skilled, savvy, and successful boys.

(Lynch 2000)

We have previously seen that Turkle's three basic criteria of the original hacking ethos were:

1 *Simplicity* the act has to be simple but impressive
2 *Mastery* the act involves sophisticated technical knowledge
3 *Illicitness* the act is 'against the rules'.

These criteria have been re-engineered by both technolibertarians and hacktivists. The former adhere to a political philosophy pared down to neo-Darwinist fundamentals. Mastery of detailed technological knowledge is displayed by realising its commercial value, and there is a provocative element to their anti-communitarian ethos. Opposed to this, the political agenda of hacktivists contains some roughly similar elements. On the one hand, their technologically inspired subversions are frequently simple and their effectiveness results from mass participation. But on the other hand, they maintain detailed technical knowledge through which they politicise the equation of technological means and ends while explicitly opposing the emerging informational inequalities of globalisation.

The crucial differences between hacking and hacktivism are also illustrated in relation to Turkle's concepts of hard and soft mastery. Technolibertarian culture exhibits hard mastery tendencies in its Wild West images and extreme political philosophy. Hacktivism marks the reassertion of soft mastery with its much more 'conversationally' based and inclusive social agenda. Hacktivism attempts to reunite the abstract 'objective' coded world of abstract capitalism with the political conditions of the real world. Unlike programmers who seek the 'crystalline purity' of code, they willingly engage with messy contingency. In contrast to hacking's politically conservative, parasitic and ultimately solipsistic form of 'personalized amateurism/autism', hacktivism manages to avoid the worst instrumental excesses of the hacker mentality but at the same time can claim to be true to hacking's primary features of ingenious re-appropriation and re-engineering. Hacktivism uses technical ingenuity not for its own sake nor does it succumb to manipulations of systems that stem from love of systemic manipulations, rather, it seeks to hack not systems, but the system itself.

7 The dot.communist manifesto

Introduction

> A sense of our mutual interdependency combined with the means for communicating across distance is producing new forms of cultural/political alliance and solidarity . . . the global perspective of the new 'social movements' may prove to be embryonic forms of a wider, more powerful order of social resistance to the repressive acts of globalization.
>
> (Tomlinson 1999: 30)

> Given increasing computer prevalence and the fact our political opponents are among the most wired in the world, it is foolish to ignore the computer. Rather, it is important to turn our attention toward the computer, to understand it, and to transform it into an instrument of resistance. For the luddites of the world who resist computers, consider using computers to resist.
>
> (Wray 1998: 1)

In the previous chapters we have seen how hacktivism can only be fully understood within the context both of its hacking heritage and of new, innovative political responses to the communication networks of viral societies. In this chapter we will conclude our analysis by looking more closely at, first, the theoretical implications of this response and, second, hacktivism's manifestos as voiced by such prominent groups as the EDT. We build upon our earlier examination of the Web (see Chapter 2) as a means of conceptualising the difference between systemic logic and new forms of oppositional, performative logic. We also build upon our already detailed accounts of hacktivism in action. This provides a context for our argument that hacktivism represents a potentially interesting new form of social action which, through its particular qualities, promises to avoid the pitfalls of previous technology-based countercultural movements while, as Tomlinson indicates above, managing to re-appropriate global communication tendencies for its own ends.

Hardt and Negri provide an interesting take on our previous discussion of the parasitical nature of hacking's relationship to technology. They argue that the power of Empire is a 'negative residue, the fallback of the operation of the multitude; it is a parasite that draws its vitality from the multitude's capacity to create ever new sources of energy and value. A parasite that saps the strength of its host, however, can endanger its own existence' (Hardt and Negri 2000: 361). From this perspective the strong trends towards parasitism and commercial co-option throughout the various generations of hackers merely represents the embodiment of the essentially parasitical characteristics of the system as a whole. Meanwhile, Wray's neo-luddite call-to-arms, cited above, advocates embracing the computer as a tool of resistance while avoiding this type of envelopment within its systems.

Latour's Prince

> The duplicity we have to understand is no longer in Princes and Popes who break their word, but in the simultaneous appeal to human and non-human allies. To the age-old passions, treacheries and stupidity of men or women, we have to add the obstinacy, the cunning, the strength of electrons, microbes, atoms, computers, missiles. Duplicity indeed, since the Princes always have two irons in the fire: one to act on human allies, the other to act on non-human allies. In brief, threatened democrats who had to fight for centuries against machinations, have now, in addition, to find their way through machines.
>
> (Latour 1988: 21)

> We should be done once and for all with the search for an outside, a standpoint that imagines a purity for our politics. It is better both theoretically and practically to enter the terrain of Empire and confront its homogenizing and heterogenizing flows in all their complexity, grounding our analysis in the power of the global multitude.
>
> (Hardt and Negri 2000: 46)

In the work of Latour, and more explicitly in Hardt and Negri, there are calls for a more sophisticated recognition of, and engagement with, the nature of power within advanced technological systems. In a relatively unacknowledged paper 'The Prince for Machines as Well as for Machinations' Latour uses and reinterprets Machiavelli's notion of the Prince(s) to argue that the distributed and ubiquitous nature of contemporary technologies requires us to adapt and modify our traditional notions of power. In an early version of themes repeated in his later work, Latour argues that science and technology are now the real sites where power and politics effectively take place. Given this basic aspect of politics in a technological age, it becomes necessary, in a similar fashion to Wray's neo-luddites, for those with social and political agendas to reorient themselves: 'that is, to penetrate where society and science are simultaneously defined through the same stratagems. This is where the new Princes stand. This is where we should stand if the Prince is to be more than a few individuals, if it is to be called "the People"' (Latour 1988: 38–9). Latour's implicit concern about the concentrated nature (the 'few individuals') of the Princes' power anticipates Hardt and Negri's concept of Empire where: 'Along with the global market and global circuits of production has emerged a global order, a new logic and structure of rule – in short, a new form of sovereignty. Empire is the political subject that effectively regulates these global exchanges, the sovereign power that governs the world' (Hardt and Negri 2000: xi).

In relation to Gunkel's notion of parasitism, Latour calls for closer attention to be paid to the imbrication of technical and non-technical:

> If 'technology' appears to have an inside it is because it has an outside. More exactly, society and technology are two sides of the same Machiavellian ingenuity. This is why, instead of the empty distinction between social ties and technical bonds, we prefer to talk of association. To the twin question 'is it social?/is it technical?' we prefer to ask 'is this association stronger or weaker than that one?'
> (Latour 1988: 27)

For the purposes of this book this emphasis upon the concept of associations is an important one. It fits with Hardt and Negri's analysis that identifies two aspects of the new conceptualisation of social networks: they are deconstructive of the '*historia rerum gestarum*, of the spectral reign of globalized capitalism' (Hardt and Negri 2000: 48);

they are constructive of new possibilities and alternative approaches. To describe a reverse engineering of globalising trends, Hardt and Negri use similar language to that we used in the portrayal of the viral spread of capitalism in Chapter 2: 'Rather than thinking of struggles as relating to one another like links in a chain, it might be better to conceive of them as communicating like a virus that modulates its form to find in each context an adequate host' (Hardt and Negri 2000: 51).

It is the dispersed and abstract nature of the new power forms that make the use of such deliberately anachronistic terms as Princes and Empire thought provoking and potentially useful. Conventional historical concepts are used to reconceptualise an essential political problem recognised within hacktivist manifestos: 'minds are melded to screenal reality, and an authoritarian power emerges that thrives on absence. The new geography is a virtual geography, and the core of political and cultural resistance must assert itself in this electronic space' (CAE 1994: 3). Such hacktivist assertions are complemented by theoretically informed assessments of globalisation that highlight what Tomlinson refers to as complex connectivity: 'By this I mean that globalization refers to the rapidly developing and ever-densening network of interconnections and interdependences that characterize modern social life' (Tomlinson 1999: 2). A common theme of numerous theoretical approaches from across the political spectrum is their emphasis upon the simultaneously abstract and pervasive effects of the new global order and the qualitatively new social conditions it gives rise to, which we explored in detail throughout Chapter 2. In this context, different forms of hacktivism mark an imaginative reinterpretation and experimentation with the otherwise dominant forces of globalisation.

The Prince in postmodernity

from our postmodern perspective the terms of the Machiavellian manifesto seem to acquire a new contemporaneity. Straining the analogy with Machiavelli a little, we could pose the problem in this way: How can productive labor dispersed in various networks find a center? How can the material and immaterial production of the brains and bodies of the many construct a common sense and direction, or rather, how can the endeavor to bridge the distance between the formation of the multitude as subject and the constitution of a democratic political apparatus find its prince?

(Hardt and Negri 2000: 64–5)

For Hardt and Negri, postmodernity represents a period when Marx's vision of the non-alienated, productive worker is further away than ever before. To add to this fundamental political problem is the possibility that the theoretical tools used to address the problem may lag behind the new postmodern forms assumed and adopted by the powers of domination. One particular irony may be that the very forms and 'fragmented subjectivities' celebrated by theorists as contributing to the death of the meta-narratives of traditional power structures merely prove to be the Machiavellian way in which Empire continues to exert its power in a new guise; the Prince remains one step ahead. For Lash too, the Prince is busy reinventing his power:

> In technological forms of life, not just resistance but also power is nonlinear. Power itself is no longer primarily pedagogical or narrative but instead, itself performative. 'Nation' now works less through 'narrative' or 'pedagogy' but through the performativity of information and communication. Power works less through the linearity and the reflective argument of discourse or ideology than through the immediacy of information, of communications.
>
> (Lash 2002: 25)

Hardt and Negri claim that in practice there is no longer any outside from which opposition to the capitalist process can be launched and as such traditional politics is effectively defunct. Their proposed solutions return us to the inside/outside configurations of power we explored in the discussion of parasitism in Chapter 6 and which Lash discusses in terms of the information economy's immanence. Empire is a non-place where exploitation is nevertheless very real and its power is expressed through its immanent nature:

> *The novelty of the new information infrastructure is the fact that it is embedded within and completely immanent to the new production processes.* At the pinnacle of contemporary production, information and communication are the very commodities produced; the network itself is the site of both production and circulation.
>
> (Hardt and Negri 2000: 298, emphasis in original)

In Hardt and Negri's account, drawing heavily if impiously on Foucault, a form of *biopower* results from the fact that capitalism has extended its interests beyond mere production. Biopolitics describes the way in which more and more parts of cultural life become susceptible to commodified influences and values. In contrast to the ambivalent, parasitical status of the hacker, biopolitics allows new forms of social militancy to arise within capital's circuits.

> Here is the strong novelty of militancy today: it repeats the virtues of insurrectional action of two hundred years of subversive experience, but at the same time it is linked to a new world, a world that knows no outside. *It knows only an inside*, a vital and ineluctable participation in the set of social structures, with no possibility of transcending them. This inside is the productive cooperation of mass intellectuality and *affective networks*, the productivity of postmodern biopolitics.
>
> (Hardt and Negri 2000: 413, emphasis added)

The circulation of struggle using capitalism's own circuits has much earlier precedents in the Internationalism of socialist movements, but there are also differences. Hardt and Negri argue for the need to update Marx's figure of the mole that actively burrows and only comes to the surface periodically at times of open class struggle: 'Well, we suspect that Marx's old mole has finally died. It seems to us, in fact, that in the contemporary passage to Empire, the structured tunnels of the mole have been replaced by the infinite undulations of the snake' (Hardt and Negri 2000: 57–8). The snake replaces Marx's mole because the depth required for subterranean burrowing has been replaced by the virtual, dispersed surfaces of the Empire's postmodern network. Hacktivism represents a good example of both Hardt and Negri's and Latour's theories in action because it innately favours laterally dispersed, socio-technical associations rather than the hierarchical privileging of the social over the technical or vice versa. However, both the Network in Latourian Actor Network Theory and the snake in the Empire may in their turn need to be conceptualised further to take into account the true significance of the information order's immanent properties. The concept of the network may be usefully revisited and re-informed by the concept of the Prince and his Empire but those seeking to conceive of new oppositional approaches increasingly make use of the notion of the web.

Information critique: neo-tribes in the Web

> There is no escaping from the information order, thus the critique of information will have to come from inside the information itself.
>
> (Lash 2002: vii)

> This is a matter of meeting information authority with information disturbance; it is direct autonomous action, suitable to the situation. One electronic affinity group could do instantly what the many could not over time. This is postmodern civil disobedience: it requires democratic interpretation of a problem, but without large-scale action. In early capital, the only power base for marginal groups was defined by their numbers. This is no longer true. Now there is a technological power base, and it is up to cultural and political activists to think it through. As time fragments, populist movements and specialized forces can work successfully in tandem. It is a matter of choosing the strategy that best fits the situation, and of keeping the techniques of resistance open.
>
> (CAE 1994: 140)

If thought of as an actual web, rather than just an alliterative catch phrase, the World Wide Web provides a radical environment for immanent forms of protest to match the new non-place of the Empire's power. To this extent, hacktivism not only represents the direct hands-on quality of the original hacker ethic but also a more enlightened form of its affinity with capitalism's abstract systems. Drawing upon McLuhan's (1964) provocative conceptualisation of electronic technologies as humanity's extended nervous system, Lash extends Latour's notion of association and its emphasis upon the inextricable nature of human, non-human bonds.

> In the immanentist technological culture subjects and objects converge in ontological status: the subject is so to speak downwardly mobile and the object upwardly mobile . . . subjects and objects fuse. . . . When technology, when the media, are extensions of the central nervous system, linear causation is deserted for a flattened, immanent world.
>
> (Lash 2002: 178)

Dyer-Witheford also presents the new immanent information order as a potentially rich environment for counter-capitalist forces that have successfully managed to adapt to its abstract nature.

> These initiatives proceed without central focus. They constitute a diffuse coalescence of microactivisms contesting the macrologic of capitalist globalization. . . . They exist as a sort of fine mist of international activism, composed of innumerable droplets of contact and communication, condensing in greater or lesser densities and accumulations, dispersing again, swirling into unexpected formations and filaments, blowing over and around the barriers dividing global workers.
>
> (Dyer-Witheford 1999: 157)

Maffesoli (1996) uses the empathy-based concept of the neo-tribe to describe in less ethereal terms the way in which, despite the prevalence of mediated environments, communitarian social behaviour can exist and indeed prosper. The neo element stems from the fact that: 'in contrast to the stability induced by classical tribalism, neo-tribalism is characterized by fluidity, occasional gatherings and dispersal' (Maffesoli 1996: 76). Throughout *The Time of the Tribes*, Maffesoli uses language resonant of both Hardt and Negri's affective networks and their image of the undulating snake claiming that: 'a shifting terrain requires quick movements; there is therefore no shame in "surfing" over the waves of sociality' (Maffesoli 1996: 5). A danger for Hardt and Negri, however, results from the fact that horizontal chains of political action may be supplanted in the era of global communication by 'vertical media events' that jump from local conditions into the focus of the global media. The global media have their passing obsessions with which to divert their viewers but meaningful, sustained attention to the local conditions that gave rise to the spectacle in the first place tends to be lost as the media move on to fresh vertical events from elsewhere.

There is evidence, however, that a more positive relationship can be constructed between the horizontal and the vertical. Dominguez suggested that the circulation of struggle occurs:

> via a strange chaos moving horizontally, nonlinearly, and over many sub-networks. Rather than operating through a central command structure in which information filters down from the top in a

vertical and linear manner . . . information about Zapatistas on the Internet has moved laterally from node to node.

(Dominguez in Fusco 1999)

Contra Hardt and Negri, it is possible that online mediated social movements can in fact use the Net for both vertical and horizontal shifts.

radical alternative media generally serve two overriding purposes: a) to express opposition vertically from subordinate quarters directly at the power structure and against its behaviour; b) to build support, solidarity, and networking laterally against policies or even against the very survival of the power structure. In any given instance, both vertical and lateral purposes may be involved.

(Downing 2001: xi)

Sasha Costanza-Chock's practice as a community arts activist provides a good illustration of how such theories might be working in practice, when the vertical and the lateral are combined so that local and wider interests are conflated in both online and physical protests.

Well it's important that it's decentralized, non-hierarchical, international. Loose but able to come together tightly in action . . . it's important to recognize that many of the actions I'd like to focus on as electronic activism are not a 'lone hacktivist' or even a small cell working together; instead these actions require the participation of hundreds, or thousands, of people to be effective. . . . Part of the difference lies in what might be called the 'moral pressure' you're able to exert; it's multiplied by the number of people involved. You're making clear to power that your action, your cause, is a popular one. In addition, you have all these people collectively mobilizing, engaging in action together, telling their friends, discussing what's happening, taking heart that they're not alone in what they feel is a struggle against injustice. So you have the movement-building elements; these same people may be inspired to go out and organize other actions, teach others about the situation, etc. Finally, you have the legal ramifications. If I set up my machine to send thousands of messages into navy.com [an event he took part in to protest against US Navy bombings in Vieques], and I cause some kind of disruption, the navy has a clear cut case against me. I knowingly and purposefully disrupted a government

> site. But if hundreds or thousands of people engage in the action, responsibility shifts. The way we set up the navy.com action, no single participating person did anything that could be construed as disrupting the site. But all those people together created a significant disruption, in fact we would've crashed it if we didn't stop. . . . During the Harvard Living Wage campaign last year I organized a virtual sit-in targeting corporate sites of 9 corporations who have board members sitting on the Harvard Board of Overseers. Communications Workers of America, representing 750,000 telecom workers, joined in.
>
> (Costanza-Chock, email interview 2001)

Hardt and Negri question: 'how can the endeavor to bridge the distance between the formation of the multitude as subject and the constitution of a democratic political apparatus find its prince?' (Hardt and Negri 2000: 65). For them, like Lash, the answer lies in finding an answer to the inside/outside question: 'any postmodern liberation must be achieved within this world, on the plane of immanence, with no possibility of any even utopian outside. The form in which the political should be expressed as subjectivity today is not clear at all' (Hardt and Negri 2000: 65). Hacktivism's integration of the vertical and the lateral, the grounded local situation and the empathetic energy of the mass intellect begin to offer at least partial answers to these questions. At this point, however, we turn to some of the factors that threaten any such project.

Resisting recuperation and the mortal dose of publicity

> Exciting pictures of Basque activists scaling the Millenium Dome in Greenwich, London may contribute to an 'innovative and variegated type of politics' but only because as a spectacle their antics are suitable for the sign-off slot at the end of prime-time news. Full of energy and eclat, this sort of media event may still constitute a withdrawal of energy from traditional domains of citizen action and produce no substantive gain for its perpetrators.
>
> (Axford and Huggins 2001: 9)

We have previously seen the recuperative, co-optive power of the system through its contribution to the alienation of microserfs. Even those less amenable to the charms of the corporate campus, however, remain vulnerable to the deflection and distortion of their attempted message. In Umberto Eco's short essay 'Towards a Semiological Guerilla Warfare' he tackles directly such problems faced by political protest in a media-dominated age. He distinguishes between a strategic and tactical approach. A strategic approach works within existing channels of communication and changes their effects by attempting to revise their content. The tactical approach, in contrast, is more confrontational. Eco views the strategic approach's likelihood of success as limited because, while it may achieve good short-term political or economic results, 'I begin to fear it produces very skimpy results for anyone hoping to restore to human beings a certain freedom in the face of the total phenomenon of Communication' (Eco 1987: 142). Using the example of the French student protests in 1968, Baudrillard's analysis questions whether the tactical approach is likely to fare any better. He suggests that the tactical approach risks being subsumed by the regime of what (similar to Eco's technological communication) he calls total communication: 'trans-gression and subversion never get "on the air" without being subtly negated as they are: transformed into models, neutralized into signs, they are eviscerated of their meaning . . . there is no better way to reduce it than to administer it a mortal dose of publicity' (Baudrillard 1981: 173–4).

It is true that some hacktivist acts are explicitly designed to make the vertical jump into the global media's consciousness. An important feature of them, as already outlined by Constanza-Chock, however, is their mass quality. The ongoing maintenance of hacktivism's mass nature combined with attempts to ground such mass actions in local conditions serves to reinforce hacktivism's overtly political motivations in the minds of both its practitioners and its witnesses. This may seem to be a reference to mass action hacktivism but we can also point to the way that even though the digitally correct work in small groups they produce tools available to a mass and which sometimes will only be successful if a mass participates (e.g. in the construction of 'server clouds'). This means that there is at least some protection against the ability of the media to successfully administer a 'mortal dose of publicity' as well as an obvious inoculation against an excessive identification with the technical means of the protest over its end. These two aspects are a path to co-option by the system being opposed. According to Constanza-Chock:

This is always the case under the logic of advanced capitalism. Already there are commercials for a soft drink that depict hordes of angry protestors facing off with riot police. All very sanitized and all the people are good-looking. But someone pulls out this soda and everything stops, all eyes are on the soda, everyone bursts into cheers. But that's only the sanitized image of what's going on in the streets of Seattle, Washington, Philadelphia, Genoa, and on and on. And if there are corporate appropriations of electronic protest tools and techniques, as there inevitably will be, it doesn't invalidate them as long as they are used as tools and techniques. Once people start hinging their identity on such things, it's dangerous, because their identity will indeed become bound up with the corporate appropriation – even if it's only because they will spend energy resisting the colonization of their 'hacker' identity. So don't hang your hat on tools, on tactics, don't romanticize this, get engaged with the broad and deep history of humanity's struggle for justice.

(Costanza-Chock, email interview 2001)

Costanza-Chock emphasises the need for selectivity in approaching technology in contrast to the seduction and over-identification exhibited by some hackers. Superficially active but ultimately passive obeisance to the complexity and thrill of exploring/surfing the matrix is avoided by not 'hanging one's hat on tools' but at the same time being fully prepared to use those tools for strategic purposes. A second route is to engage aggressively with the political nature of tools, as digitally correct hacktivists do, although this faces the problem of simply deepening the focus on the tool. These two approaches to an oppositional cyberpolitics somewhat redefine Eco's previous concepts of strategic and tactical resistance in the face of technological communication and seeks to grapple positively with Baudrillard's pessimistic concept of total communication along with calls to enter into the new, fluid terrains of power. A further key feature of hacktivism's ability to avoid systemic recuperation is the extent to which its ethos and actions are informed by a non-rationalist, performative element, to which we now turn.

The rise of the hacktivist ethic and the dot.communist manifesto: reclaiming the agora

The paradigm of the network can then be seen as the re-actualization of the ancient myth of community; myth in the sense in which something that has perhaps never really existed acts, effectively, on the imagination of the time. This explains the existence of those small tribes, ephemeral in their actualization, but which nevertheless create a state of mind that, for its part, seems called upon to last. Must we see this then as the tragic and cyclical return of the same? It is possible, however, that it forces us to rethink the mysterious relationship uniting 'place' and 'we'. For, although it does not fail to annoy the upholders of institutional knowledge, the jarring and imperfect everyday life inescapably secretes a true 'everyday knowledge' ('co-naissance') that the subtle Machiavelli called the 'thinking of the public square'.

(Maffesoli 1996: 148)

Maffesoli's consideration of the novel qualities of neo-tribes highlights the non-institutional nature of the knowledge and empathetic networks that they create. In relation to our previous discussion about the possibilities of oppositional groups managing to get inside the palace of the Prince/Emperor, *the thinking of the public square* points in an interesting direction. It is true that strategies of subversion are often co-opted and there is a common theme within the work of Hardt and Negri, Latour, and Lash that such co-option takes quickly changing and highly adaptable forms. It is also true, however, that such neutralisation of subversion tends to occur through the application of 'the bourgeois aesthetic of efficiency' (CAE 1994: 12). The absorption of hackers into the microserf mentality was premised upon a redirection of their love of code into a love of commercially viable code. Even if politically motivated hackers sought to use code for rebellious or disruptive purposes, we have already seen how such desires quickly begin to sit uncomfortably with their parasitical dependence upon the system: there is a limit to how underground the computer underground can in fact go.

We are living through some of the most interesting times, in which the efflorescence of the lived gives rise to a pluralistic knowledge, in which disjunctive analysis, the techniques of separation and conceptual a priorism are giving way to a complex phenomenology which can integrate participation, description, life narratives and the varied manifestations of collective imaginations.

(Maffesoli 1996: 155)

In contrast, hacktivism represents a practical illustration of Maffesoli's general call for the promotion of an underground social power that is not as susceptible to recuperation. This is the 'complex phenomenology' that makes use of the 'collective imaginations' that appear similar to Hardt and Negri's mass intellect. Unlike the computer underground's ultimately conservative affinity with the system, hacktivism's emphasis upon the performative fulfils Maffesoli's call.

> To restate a situationist expression, rather than 'fighting alienation with alienated methods' (bureaucracy, political parties, militancy, deferment of pleasure), one uses derision, irony, laughter – all underground strategies which undermine the process of normalization and domestication which are the goals of the guarantors of the external and hence abstract order.
>
> (Maffesoli 1996: 50)

For the EDT, the technical aspects of political protests, on which the media invariably fixate, are in fact the least important part of a larger and more significant three-act social performance that constitutes their hacktivism. Ricardo Dominguez calls this performance a social drama. The first act involves stating what is going to happen and its political purpose, the second is the act itself, and the third is the subsequent dialogue and discussion that is created. In this way he argues: 'A virtual plaza, a digital situation, is thus generated in which we all gather and have an encounter, or an Encuentro, as the Zapatistas would say – about the nature of neo-liberalism in the real world and in cyberspace' (Dominguez in Fusco 1999). This may be one form of a radicalised public square, in Maffesoli's sense. Digital Zapatismo's social drama also includes periods of tactical silence where, literally in Mexico and metaphorically online, both real-world and internet-based activists retreat back into the jungle for a period of calm reflection. This deliberately contrasts with the conventional mass media's need for constant noise.

As we have seen, there has been a certain Latin American influence upon hacktivism which we could perhaps term 'practical magic realism'. For example, the Digital Zapatismo's activity is informed by Mayan culture and they try to draw connections between such influences and rebellious strands that exist deep within western traditions (Dominguez 1999). Seeking to re-engineer capitalist code does not mean the process has to be humourless: 'The body without organs is Ronald McDonald, not an esoteric aesthetic; after all, there is a critical place for comedy and humor as a means of resistance. Perhaps this is the Situationist

International's greatest contribution to the postmodern aesthetic. The dancing Nietzsche lives' (CAE 1994: 20). We might suggest that the bears who appear on your screen smiling and laughing when they are transmitting information within peek-a-booty or appear with their mouths taped over when they are digitally silent, are demonstrating the possibilities of Nietzschean networked dancing, including its potential failures. Ricardo Dominguez of the EDT sees a 'dancing Nietzsche' in hacktivism in terms of Diogenes and his rejection of Plato's rationalism. From this perspective, Hardt and Negri's contemporary abstract power of Empire and Latour's re-evaluation of Machiavelli's Prince, as well as the previously cited rhetorical excesses of the technolibertarian Wild West, all have their earliest origins in Platonic thought. In an analysis that shares aspects with the Frankfurt School's notion of the dialectic of enlightenment, the obsessive hacker love of code can be seen as the contemporary fulfilment of a rationalist project as old as Western culture itself:

> Our digital condition often embarks the ship of dematerialization, always seeking that final perfect Orphic state of transmigration. The final download of all realities into an endless ethernet of the extropic dream. Plato was always already on-line clicking out the Socratic agenda of our future state: the Virtual Republic. A Republic of geometric perfection, immortal mind children, and the rational discourse of dialectics. . . . In the Virtual Republic there will be no music, no theater, no painting, all email from Dionysus will be filtered out from the listserves. Who and what can piss against this hegemonic code? The Pantomimic Materialist, or become a dog network. Perhaps the only tactical gestures capable of disturbing the total emergence of the incorporeal state can come from the performative matrix of Diogenes on-line. To heed his call for public actions in the middle of the marketplace that break open the Virtual Republic with somatic-networks. . . . Diogenes on-line refuses to be reduced to physiognomic silence before the endless onslaught of digital perfection. We must become dogs that dig holes between the holy trinity code, connectivity and networks.
>
> (Dominguez undated)

In contemporary Western society the logos of Greek rationality has been replaced by corporate logos. There remain ample opportunities for resistance, however, ranging from Klein's and Lash's hopes that activist spiders will weave their webs around the shiny corporate networks to more performative attempts to recapture Diogenes' wilful spirit of rebellion. Marx identified a basic tension of capitalism in its continual need for expansion. Global capital exploits on a world scale but is also vulnerable to new socio-technical associations that make use of that same cosmopolitan quality capital's circuits promote. The sense developed by hacktivism is that advanced communication circuits can be more than just relatively neutral and empty conduits within which struggle as well as capital can circulate. There is a desire to create new forms of culturally rich living spaces with which to counter the sterile homogeneity of code: 'It is not impossible to imagine that, correlatively with technological developments, the growth in urban tribes has encouraged a "computerized palaver" that assumes the rituals of the ancient agora [public square]?' (Maffesoli 1996: 25). Or, put another way: 'We do not lack communication, on the contrary we have too much of it. We lack creation. We lack resistance to the present' (Deleuze and Guattari cited in Hardt and Negri 2000: 393). The various techniques of the EDT and other hacktivist groups are replacing the corporate slogans of essentially empty commodity value with positive social activity, while the actions of some, such as Cult of the Dead Cow, ensure spaces remain open to alternative ways in cyberspace. For Marx, the flip side of capital's spread is a concomitant decline in parochialism and all its implied conservatism: 'And as in material production, so also in intellectual production. The intellectual creations of individual nations become common property. National one-sidedness and narrow-mindedness become more and more impossible, and from the numerous national and local literatures, there arises a world literature' (Marx and Engels 1972: 476–7).

In the following extract we quote Dominguez at length to give a full flavour of the manifesto he advocates; an alternative vision whereby hacktivism can reclaim social space drawing upon the vibrant strengths of the ancient agora and allying them with the technologically facilitated possibilities of postmodern sociality.

> The idea of a virtual republic in Western Civilization can be traced back to Plato, and is connected to the functions of public space. The Republic incorporated the central concept of the Agora. The Agora was the area for those who were entitled to engage in rational discourse of Logos, and to articulate social policy as the Law, and thus contribute to the evolution of Athenian democracy. Of course

those who did speak were, for the most part, male, slave-owning and ship-owning merchants, those that represented the base of Athenian power. We can call them Dromos: those that belong to the societies of speed. Speed and the Virtual Republic are the primary nodes of Athenian democracy – not much different than today. The Agora was constantly being disturbed by Demos, what we would call those who demonstrate or who move into the Agora and make gestures. Later on, with the rise of Catholicism – Demos would be transposed into Demons, those representatives of the lower depths. Demos did not necessarily use the rational speech of the Agora, they did not have access to it; instead, they used symbolic speech or a somatic poesis – Nomos. In the Agora, rational speech is known as Logos. The Demos gesture is Nomos, the metaphorical language that points to invisibility, that points to the gaps in the Agora. The Agora is thus disturbed; the rational processes of its codes are disrupted, the power of speed was blocked. EDT alludes to this history of Demos as it intervenes with Nomos. The Zapatista FloodNet injects bodies as Nomos into digital space, a critical mass of gestures as blockage. What we also add to the equation is the power of speed is now leveraged by Demos via the networks. Thus Demos qua Dromos create the space for a new type of social drama to take place. Remember in Ancient Greece, those who were in power and who had slaves and commerce, were the ones who had the fastest ships. EDT utilizes these elements to create drama and movement by empowering contemporary groups of Demos with the speed of Dromos – without asking societies of command and control for the right to do so. We enter the Agora with the metaphorical gestures of Nomos and squat on high speed lanes of the new Virtual Republic – this creates a digital platform or situation for a techno-political drama that reflects the real condition of the world beyond code. This disturbs the Virtual Republic that is accustomed to the properties of Logos, the ownership of property, copyright, and all the different strategies in which they are attempting enclosure of the Internet.

(Dominguez cited in Fusco 1999)

This provides a vivid articulation of hacktivism's non-parasitical use of the network for uncircumscribed, non-commodified purposes. It is in keeping with the various theoretical injunctions we have seen that promote the need to develop a more sophisticated understanding of the changing nature of power within technologically complex structures. Dominguez seeks to retain the rebellious vitality of Diogenes, but with a full awareness that without a developed Machiavellian understanding of technologically mediated power, the network risks becoming an expansive but nevertheless ultimately circumscribing barrel.

Conclusion

> One can only call the political impact of 'globalization' the pathology of over-diminished expectations ... we have a myth which exaggerates the degree of our helplessness in the face of contemporary economic forces.
>
> (Hirst and Thompson cited in Tomlinson 1999: 16)

> Movements in complex societies are disenchanted prophets. ... Movements are a sign; they are not merely an outcome of the crisis, the last throes of a passing society. They signal a deep transformation in the logic and the processes that guide complex societies. ... Contemporary movements are prophets of the present. What they possess is not the force of the apparatus but the power of the word. They announce the commencement of change; not, however, a change in the distant future but one that is already a presence. They force the power out into the open and give it a shape and a face. They speak a language that seems to be entirely their own, but they say something that transcends their particularity and speaks to us all.
>
> (Melucci 1996: 1)

Globalisation, along with terms such as information society or networked society, has become the *bête noire* of contemporary political discourse. Too often globalisation is portrayed in deterministic terms that question the viability of resistance to its powerful effects yet also posit globalisation as having remote and difficult to control causes. Despite hacking's innate countercultural potential, we have seen how hacking evinced relatively little radical activity to challenge this largely pessimistic political status quo, despite (or perhaps because) it exists at the heart of a global medium. Hackers' over-identification with technical means over political ends and their parasitical relationship to various technological systems means that although they are at the heart of the exercise of power, they remain in an ultimately powerless dependent relationship.

We have seen in this chapter how the hacktivist movement, in contrast, has no such ends–means confusion. The key significance of hacktivism is the performative manner with which it imaginatively allies technology-based techniques with non-commodified practices. It rejects the microserf mentality that represented 'the first full-scale integration of the corporate realm into the private' (Coupland 1995: 211) and reclaims the demos from its co-option within the limited communication models of Western liberal democracy. Whether by promoting open source software whose function is to challenge the control of nation-states over what their citizens are and are not allowed to know or by initiating three-act dramas, during which discussion is both promoted and websites attacked and closed down, hacktivism is a politics that lives and dies by its informational intimacies. Mass action hacktivists reject commodification and resist the assumption they must use cyberspatial technologies according to norms of efficiency set by capitalist, viral societies. Digitally correct hacktivists overcome a narrow identification of means and ends in terms of abstract technological systems and assert a powerful politicisation of such systems. Both are part of hacktivism and hacktivism is a pure informational politics for informational times.

8 Hacktivism

Informational politics for informational times

'ISMO!': Hacktivismo and Digital Zapatismo

The 'ismo' in Hacktivismo and Digital Zapatismo is important, it points to the common roots of hacktivists in struggles around and resistance to twenty-first-century dominations and exploitations. Hacktivismo began as a 'special operations group' including several members of Cult of the Dead Cow, and its first major project was peek-a-booty. Hacktivismo launched and runs Six/Four, the anti-censorship, anti-national firewall software. Digital Zapatismo is (another) articulation by Ricardo Dominguez of how to hack the future by creating electronic civil disobedience. Both Digital Zapatismo and Hacktivismo, by their use of 'ismo', point back to hacktivism's roots in, specifically, the Zapatista struggle and, more broadly, protest in informational, viral times. We will turn back to these two 'ismo's in the next section, but recognising their common roots draws our gaze back to the birthplace of hacktivism.

We now have a view of hacktivism in total. We have seen how a point of intersection between hacking, viral times and millennial protests wrought a new movement. A virtual movement that simultaneously contests viral capitalism's tendency to abstraction in the service of an ever more intrusive commodification and promotes access to information through the generation of tools that struggle to keep cyberspace free of corporate and state domination. It is worthwhile at this stage to recall these three contexts: hacking, viral societies, protest.

Hackers form a community at home with, if not obsessed with, demonstrating mastery of the abstractions of code in cyberspace. We briefly traced the history of this community, noting how its original radical impulses were undermined both by a corporate recuperation and the self-absorbed destructions and internal contests of crackers. In

Chapter 6, we explored the consequences of this drift in a community which conflates means and ends in relation to technical systems and consequently can render services to some of the worst tendencies of twenty-first-century societies. We saw the machismo and bodily-hate that emerged within hacking. At the same time, we saw how hacktivism, having been born within hacking, was now reflecting back onto it the need to re-politicise its increasingly arid obsessions with mastery.

The regressions of hacking are intertwined, as both cause and effect, with the emergence of informational, viral societies. We can now recall this context for hacktivism of the broad societal shifts variously called the emergence of information or networked societies, of advanced capitalism or complex societies or of globalisation. We explored this tangle of different approaches to the one phenomenon – the restructuring or worldwide socio-economies at the end of the twentieth century – by adopting the metaphor of the virus. This allowed us to draw out some of the key elements for hacktivism of socio-economic changes and, in particular, to see the way capitalism's century-old drive towards commodification has played a key role in both the generation of immaterial commodities and the acceleration of existing trends to abstraction. Immateriality and abstraction are key, if not foundational, factors in the home of hacking and hacktivism – cyberspace.

The trends of viral societies are contested by alternative visions voiced most powerfully by protest movements. We traced the history of protest movements, reaching back to the emergence of industrial capitalism and racing forward to informational times. In particular, we saw the rise of the 'anti-globalisation movement' at the end of the twentieth century and its engagement with the regressive globalisation carried out by governments following a neo-liberal agenda. We explored the series of mass demonstrations carried out, usually, in developed countries and we saw the struggles of indigenous peoples, the newly urbanised and more in developing countries.

With all three of these contexts in place, we were able to see how their intersection gave rise to a unique movement that sits amidst powerful currents of our times: hacktivism. As a movement it deserves attention because it is situated where it is; drawing in powerful alternative visions of society, arming these visions with informational tools and injecting itself as a radical virus into twenty-first-century societies.

At the three-way junction we have identified arise the advocates of electronic civil disobedience and the priests of free information. Both trends within hacktivism connect to this junction, this node from which their actions spring. However, this does not mean these two trends agree or form a simple unity. In concluding this book, it will be useful to meditate a little while on the conflicts and unities of mass action and digitally correct hacktivism. This both confirms and complicates the vision of hacktivism as a movement and provides a way of summarising without simply repeating.

Two tribes

Ricardo Dominguez, as our frequent references to him and his work with EDT attest, has been a key member of early mass action hacktivism. He has been part of grounding these actions in Zapatista support and then in the anti-globalisation movement. He has gained a prominence through speaking and writing that may, at times, overemphasise his personal work but hardly ever overemphasises his role in delineating mass action hacktivism and electronic civil disobedience. For one last time in this book we turn to him, and one final quotation, in order to begin with the tribe of mass action hacktivists. Here is his conclusion to his influential piece defining Digital Zapatismo, from a section called 'hacking the future'.

> Digital Zapatismo has always been an open system of sprawling networks – this has been the force multiplier of the movement. It used digital cultures' most basic system of exchange, e-mail between people to disturb the Informatic State. Now that we know that they are using, as we always suspected, hyper-surveillance filters to regain control of the network. . . .We must begin to invent other methods of Electronic Civil Disobedience. . . . The Zapatista Networks, in the spirit of Chiapas are developing methods of electronic disturbance as sites of invention and political action for peace. At this point in time it is difficult to know how much of a disturbance these acts of electronic civil disobedience specifically make. What we do know is that neoliberal power is extremely concerned by these acts.
>
> (Dominguez 2003)

In this article, Dominguez lists several actions that need to be developed, several of which look very close to the concerns of digitally correct hacktivism. For example he talks of needing 'Alternative networks with more access and more bandwidth' (Dominguez 2003). However,

Dominguez also calls for 'spamming engines for massive email actions' (Dominguez 2003). Here he envisages a blocking attack using email. This is something contrary to the digitally correct's desire to engage in discussion and their claim there is no need to shout down anyone in cyberspace as all views can be heard at once. Thus the fault line between mass action and the digitally correct appears again. It is one we have already seen in the complaints of hackers against EDT's FloodNet and in CDC's critical response to the Electrohippies' attack on the WTO networks in Seattle. We are also in a position to see why this fault line emerges.

Mass action hacktivists do not seek to use cyberspatial technologies to their fullest extent. They engage in a paradoxical politics as they cannot operate without virtual technologies but they refuse to use them in their most obvious or 'natural' way. Hacktivists like EDT, Electro-hippies and Netstrike seek only a little virtual amplification and refuse the potential cyberspace offers to multiply their physical selves thousands and thousands of times over. They do this to ensure electronic civil disobedience claims the legitimating power of many people. Like civil disobedience, electronic civil disobedience relies for its effects on the support of a mass. In the inherently non-physical world of cyber-space, where so often it is easier to count in numbers of computers than numbers of humans, this sets mass action against the main currents of virtual life.

It is no wonder then that the digitally correct metaphorically scratch their heads over mass action hacktivism. Perhaps it is sometimes no more than a sense that mass action has misunderstood the nature of cyberspace, for example when Oxblood Ruffin points out to the Electrohippies something they surely already knew: 'The only difference between a program like Stacheldraht [a DDoS application written by The Mixter] and the client side javascript program written by the Electrohippies is the difference between blowing something up and being pecked to death by a duck' (Ruffin 2000, brackets already included). Here we can almost hear the quizzical assertion that if mass action wants to bring down a site then why not just blow it up? Cyberspace offers dynamite to pretty much anyone.

We should also not dismiss the digitally correct's complaint as a kind of elitism. The digitally correct could be thought to be looking down from the masterful heights of hacking's expertise and, with a sad nod of the head, be correcting the confusions of those below. In fact, their concern is that mass action hacktivists are inventing a politics which cannot swim in the water it wants to, that mass action hacktivists are inventing the first self-drowning politics. We might reflect whether mass action hacktivism is really engaging in effective actions or is simply playing out a desire to engage with Internet technology, even if that technology contradicts their favoured actions. We might ask: What use is an online mass action? Who knows it has occurred? Are not some of the most powerful uses of mass demonstrations – the sense of being on the march with so many others – simply absent online? There are no bystanders in cyberspace, nor can you see the people you are marching with. Is it possible that refusing cyberspace's ability to amplify while still using cyberspace means that mass action only gains virtuality's ability to distance people from each other and deepens already abstract social relations? Mass action hacktivism might, in this way, simply be inventing alienated civil disobedience, while simultaneously refusing the powers cyberspace does offer.

We might reflect that the digitally correct have better understood the use of virtuality for political protest. Perhaps their acceptance of hacking's identification of means with ends is simply an acceptance of how things work in cyberspace. If so, their attempt to re-politicise technological systems becomes an oppositional move in cyberspace. Hackers identified the means and ends of technological systems with each other, which led to a failure to deal with any politics but the abstract desire to master technical systems. The digitally correct take up these systems, these coterminous virtual means and virtual ends, and both remind us of the politics of information inherent in them and radicalise that politics. But this leads us to another point of concern: the tools created within the politicised context of digitally correct hacktivism are able to serve many different political masters. If the core political argument is that tools must be created that ensure free secure access to information, then the political opposition is not neo-liberalism or a regressive masculinity but anyone who blocks flows of information. To consider the problems that result from such a stance, we can look at Hacktivismo's response to the question of whether all information should be available – a response articulated at the time peek-a-booty was first announced.

Q: Do you think all information should be accessible?
A: No. That's why we talk about 'lawfully published' information in the Hacktivismo Declaration. Essentially that cuts out things like legitimate government secrets, kiddie porn, matters of personal

privacy, and other accepted restrictions. But even the term 'lawfully published' is full of landmines. Lawful to whom? What is lawful in the United States can get you a bullet in the head in China. At the end of the day we recognize that some information needs to be controlled. But that control falls far short of censoring material that is critical of governments, intellectual and artistic opinion, information relating to women's issues or sexual preference, and religious opinions. That's another way of saying that most information wants to be free; the rest needs a little privacy, even non-existence in the case of things like kiddie porn. Everyone will have to sort the parameters of this one out for themselves.

(CDC 2000)

The tension within this declaration is plain. Given what we have said about digitally correct politics the answer of 'no' and the claim that there are such things as 'legitimate government secrets' might seem surprising. But immediately the more expected politics makes itself felt. Who defines what is legitimate? When does a piece of information become illegitimate? This ambivalence leaves the reader with only the example of kiddie porn as information that should be restricted and even that definition of illegitimate information is undermined by the final sentence, which enunciates a kind of giving up on any restrictive qualifications relevant to the principle of free flows of information.

Here is digitally correct's weakness. If it builds systems that keep free flows of information at their maximum then any digitisable information can pass through the networks they create. Is this not simply the re-emergence of the original hacker problem we identified in which the mastery of technical systems supplants the uses those systems are put to? Is this the sniggering revenge of hacking's worst sides? We might wonder whether it is necessary to be critical of the powers of virtuality, as mass action hacktivists are, to be able to create an oppositional politics. There can be no doubt that the digitally correct seek to radicalise hacking and that they make clearer than any other group the nature and importance of a politics of information, yet the doubt must remain that information is a means not an end.

We have now touched on the internal critiques of hacktivism, which have been launched by hacktivists against hacktivists. We have focused in this conclusion so far on divisions in order to summarise and clarify. The opposition is useful because it allows precision, yet at the same time it is dangerous if it is overemphasised. All social movements engage in such internal discussions; they are more a sign of the strength in diversity some movements have than they are of internal divisions that presage failure. We can now turn, in finishing this book, to hacktivism's place as a whole, yet complex and not simply unified, movement in the politics of our times. If we live in times when information is a key resource and structuring agent, then the picture of hacktivism we have drawn is of a social movement of information.

Informational politics

In the beginning, before it was even named, there were high hopes for hacktivism.

> Enough technology has fallen between the cracks of the corporate–military hierarchy that experimentation with cell structure among resistant cultures can begin. New tactics and strategies of civil disobedience are now possible, ones that aim to disturb the virtual order, rather than the spectacular order. With these new tactics many problems could be avoided that occur when resistors use older tactics not suitable to a global context.
>
> (CAE 1994: 142–3)

These hopes now rest on hacktivism's contestation of abstraction with abstraction. If we have correctly identified in viral societies the increasing dematerialisation of cultural and social life, through the commodification of our immaterial and intimate spaces, then the radical potential of hacktivism lies primarily in its politicisation of hacking's mastery of the technologies of immaterial space. Hacktivism generates abstractions which contest abstractions fuelling the exploitations of viral societies and this unites hacktivism across its various actions.

When an action of electronic civil disobedience is run, the bodies that block are abstractions. Mass electronic civil disobedience creates the complex situation in which an embodied presence at a terminal uses the direct action to become an abstract virtual presence, which joins with other abstractions to jam up a virtual site. Legitimation comes from the embodied presence, action from the virtual presence.

The highways, even the superhighways, of cyberspace can be peopled with these ghostly presences and slowed down. The exit ramp to the WTO network, to the Mexican president's virtual home, to so many other progenitors of a regressive viralism, can be peopled with abstractions. Abstractions to block abstractions. The practical magic of hacktivism can slow and negate within cyberspace, all the time asserting its political rights through the mass of bodies sitting at terminals the world over.

When the virus propagators of nation-states or neo-liberalism begin to run scared of the abstractions of cyberspace, then the experts of virtuality can begin to tinker with the means of virtual production. Creating new forms of technology enables hacktivists to propagate different means of virtual production, ensuring abstractions amenable to hacktivist goals remain possible. The very fabric of virtual lives is constituted by technologies whose nature is contestable, but only at the level of lines of code and the hardware to run the code. Hacking gives to hacktivism a history and culture of expertise in creating, producing and distributing hacks which mould the nature of cyberspace.

The highways can be dug up, new turn-offs built and alternative routes created. The ability of individuals behind certain barriers to gain the information they want can be recreated when hacktivists take up the battle of code. Here machines for the production of oppositional abstractions are built: immaterial factories for virtual resistance. The practical magic of hacktivism can re-engineer cyberspace, creating political rights for masses of people.

No one, not even Ricardo Dominguez or Oxblood Ruffin (or us), would suggest hacktivism is perfect or has achieved its goals – even if hacktivism could define a single set of goals. This complexity of hacktivism, that we have dwelt on earlier in this chapter, is something shared with all social movements. This is networked politics, not hierarchised, institutionalised, bureaucratic and de-radicalised politics. Yet we have seen hacktivism out fighting the good virtual fight: pushing into the politics of contestation the abstractions that, within cyberspace, are the only entities capable of real conflict.

Neither is this a matter of hacktivism obsessing over online life to the exclusion of offline or in the naive belief cyberspace exists as a world unto-itself. The actions of hacktivists ultimately address the poverties and lack of human rights viral societies are reinventing. Digitally correct hacktivists are concerned with information not just out of a desire to maintain cyberspace's counter-censorship abilities, they do so because people are jailed, repressed and damaged by their nation-state's use of censorship. Mass action hacktivists are concerned to propagate mass gatherings of virtual bodies not just out of a desire to see civil disobedience and resistance at work in virtual lives, they do so in support of people who are being jailed, repressed and damaged in their virtual and non-virtual lives. Hacktivism addresses politics, virtual and non-virtual.

They are out there, to what future we cannot say. We can only point to the trends we have already identified. Not only has a rich and varied virtual social movement come into existence, but this movement has shown significant potential for re-radicalising hacking and digital cultures generally. The importance of such cultures and of cyberspace in general to the twenty-first century means hacktivists operate their politics in highly visible locations that are potentially privileged for effective action. Hacktivists represent resistance in viral times. Hacktivists are an opposition in, for and against cyberspace. Hacktivists are the first social movement of virtuality.

Notes

1 Hacking and hacktivism

1 'Phone-phreakers' is used to describe people who used various electronic devices to hack into the telephone networks to explore the system and/or obtain free phone calls.

2 Quotations in this and the subsequent section cited as interviews have previously appeared in Taylor 1999. Any subsequent interview quotations were obtained solely for the purposes of this book.

3 Hacktivism and the history of protest

1 No one of these unwieldy set of terms is adequate to distinguish the parts of the globe that in this context need to be explored separately. Though recognised as only partially adequate the terms Northern/ Southern and overdeveloped/underdeveloped will be used in this book.

4 Mass action hacktivism

1 Quotations cited as (Fusco 1999) were taken from an interview entitled, "Performance Art in a Digital Age: A Conversation with Ricardo Dominguez" that took place on Thursday 25 November 1999, at the Institute of International Visual Arts. The interview was heavily edited by Coco Fusco and transcribed by InIVA staff. It was republished in Centrodearte.com and Latinarte.com.

Bibliography

Adorno, T. (1991) *The Culture Industry*, London: Routledge.

Armitage, J. (1999) 'Resisting the Neoliberal Discourse of Technology: the politics of cyberculture in the age of the virtual class'; available at http://www.ctheory.net/text_file.asp?pick=111 (checked 23 October 2003).

Atton, C. (2002) *Alternative Media*, London: Sage.

Axford, B. and Huggins, R. (2001) *New Media and Politics*, London: Sage.

Baranowski, P. (2002) 'Codecon Presentation of Peekabooty'; available at http://www.peek-a-booty.org as both mp3 video recording of presentation and as powerpoint slides (checked 17 October 2003).

Barber, B. (2001) *Jihad vs McWorld*, New York: Ballantine.

Barlow, J. P. (1990) 'Crime and Puzzlement', *Whole Earth Review*, Fall 1990: 44–57.

Baudrillard, J. (1981) *For a Critique of the Political Economy of the Sign*, New York: Telos Press.

Bird, T. and Jordan, T. (1999) 'Sounding Out New Social Movements and the Left: interview with Stuart Hall, Doreen Massey and Michael Rustin', in Jordan, T. and Lent, A. (1999) *Storming the Millennium: the new politics of change*, London: Lawrence and Wishart: 195–215.

Boal, I. and Brooks, J. (eds) (1993) *Resisting the Virtual Life: the culture and politics of information*, San Francisco: City Lights Books.

Boorsook, P. (2000) *Cyberselfish: a critical romp through the terribly libertarian world of hi-tech*, London: Little Brown.

Bowcott, O. and Hamilton, S. (1990) *Beating the System*, London: Bloomsbury.

Brown, D. (1988) *Cybertrends: chaos, power and accountability in the Information Age*, London: Penguin.

Burke, J. and Paton, N. (2000) 'Coming to a Screen near You', *The Observer*, 7 May: 19.

CAE (1994) *The Electronic Disturbance*, New York: Autonomedia.

CAE (1996) *Electronic Civil Disobedience and Other Unpopular Ideas*, New York: Autonomedia.

Castells, M. (1997) *The Power of Identity: the Information Age*, volume 2, Oxford: Blackwell.

CDC (1999a) 'Don't Worry Windows Users, Everything Will Be BO2K: press release from Cult of the Dead Cow'; available at http://www.cultdeadcow.com

CDC (1999b) 'Cult of the Dead Cow: BO2K', Defcon 7, 1999; available at: http://www.defcon.org/html/links/defcon-media-archives.html (checked 17 October 2003).

CDC (2000) 'The Hacktivismo Faq'; available at http://www.cultdeadcow.com/cDc_files/HacktivismoFAQ.html (checked 25 October 2003).

CDC (2002) 'Camera/Shy Announcement'; available at www.cultdeadcow.com (checked 16 August 2002).

CERT (1998) *CERT Vulnerability Note VN-98.07*; available at http://www.cert.org (checked 25 October 2003).

Cherny, L. and Weise, E. (eds) (1996) *Wired Women: gender and new realities in cyberspace*, Seattle: Seal Press.

Cleaver, H. (1998) 'The Zapatistas and the Electronic Fabric of Struggle', in Holloway, J. and Pelaez, E. (eds) (1998) *Zapatista!: reinventing revolution in Mexico*, London: Pluto: 81–103.

Collier, G. (1999) *Basta!: land and the Zapatista rebellion in Chiapas*, Oakland: Food First Books.

Colligan, D. (1982) 'The Intruder – a biography of Cheshire Catalyst', *Technology Illustrated*, October/November; available at http://www.textfiles.com/news/chesire.phk (checked 23 October 2003).

Conley, V. (ed.) (1993) *Rethinking Technologies*, Minneapolis: University of Minnesota Press.

Corr, A. (1999) *No Trespassing!: squatting, rent strikes and land struggles worldwide*, Cambridge, MA: South End Press.

Costanza-Chock, S. (2001) Email interview conducted by Paul A. Taylor, September.

Count Zero (1999) 'Interview with Count Zero, member of Cult of the Dead Cow', *ABCNews.com*; available at http://www.abcnews.co.com/sections/tech/DailyNews/chat_countzero.html (checked 2 February 2001).

Coupland, D. (1995) *Microserfs*, New York: Flamingo.

Coyle, C. (1999) *The Weightless World: strategies for managing the digital economy*, Cambridge, MA: MIT Press.

Dann, J. and Dozois, G. (eds) (1996) 'Introduction', in *Hackers*, New York: Ace Books.

De Certeau, M. (1988) *The Practices of Everyday Life*, Berkeley: University of California Press.

De León, J. P. (2001) 'Travelling Back for Tomorrow', in Marcos, *Our Word is Our Weapon: selected writings Subcomandante Marcos*, London: Serpents Tail: xxiii–xxxi.

Deleuze, G. (1989) *Cinema 2: the time-image*, Minneapolis: University of Minnesota Press.

Della Porta, D. and Diani, M. (1999) *Social Movements: an introduction*, Oxford: Blackwell.

Denning, D. (1999) 'Activism, Hacktivism, and Cyberterrorism: the Internet as a tool for influencing foreign policy'; available at http://www.nautilus.org/info-policy/workshop/papers/denning.html (checked 23 October 2003).

Dominguez, R. (undated) 'Diogenes Online: gestures against the Virtual Republic', *Switch* 4(2); available at http://switch.sjsu.edu/web/v4n2/ricardo/ (checked 21 October 2003).

Dominguez, R. (1998) 'Digital Zapatismo'; available at http://www.nyu.edu/projects/wray/DigZap.html (checked 30 October 2002).

Dominguez, R. (1999) 'Post-Media Impossibilities', *Ctheory*, Even-Scene e081; available at http://www.ctheory.net (checked 24 October 2003)

Dominguez, R. (2003) 'Digital Zapatismo'; available at http://www.thing.net/~rdom/ecd/DigZap.html (checked 25 October 2003).

Downing, J. (ed.) (2001) *Radical Media: rebellious communication and social movements*, London: Sage.

Dyer-Witheford, N. (1999) *Cyber-Marx: cycles and circuits of struggle in high technology capitalism*, Illinois: University of Illinois Press.

Eco, U. (1987) *Travels in Hyperreality*, London: Picador.

EDT (1998) 'Chronology of Swarm'; available at http://www.thing.net/~rdom/ (checked 29 January 2002).

Electrohippies Collective (2000) *Client-side Distributed Denial-of-service: valid campaign tactic or terrorist act?*, Occasional Paper No.1; available at http://www.fraw.org.uk/archive/ehippies/papers/op1.html (checked 18 November 2002).

Fine, D. (1995) 'Why is Kevin Lee Poulson really in Jail?'; available at http://www.well.com/user/fine/journalism/jail.html (checked 23 October 2003).

Frank, T. (2001) *One Market Under God: extreme capitalism, market populism and the end of economic democracy*, London: Secker and Warburg.

Freedman, D. and Mann, C. (1997) *@Large: the strange case of the world's biggest internet invasion*, New York: Simon and Schuster.

Fusco, C. (1999) *Performance Art in a Digital Age: a conversation with Ricardo Dominguez*. Unpublished paper.

Gibson, S. (2001) *The Strange Tale of the Denial-of-Service Attacks Against Grc.com*; available at http://grc.com/files/grcdos.pdf (checked 18 November 2002).

Gibson, W. (1984) *Neuromancer*, London: Grafton.

Gilboa, N. (1996) 'Elites, Lamers, Narcs and Whores: exploring the computer underground', in Cherny, L. and Weise, E. (eds) (1996) *Wired Women: gender and new realities in cyberspace*, Seattle: Seal Press: 98–113.

Gilmore, J. (1996) Interview conducted by Tim Jordan, August.

Greenfeld, K. T. (1993) 'The Incredibly Strange Mutant Creatures Who Rule the Universe of Alienated Japanese Zombie Computer Nerds (Otaku to You)'; available at http://www.eff.org/pub/Net_culture/Cyberpunk/otaku.article (checked 21 October 03).

Greider, W. (1997) *One World Ready or Not*, New York: Touchstone.

Grether, R. (2000) 'How the Etoy Campaign Was Won'; available at http://www. heise.de/tp/english/inhalt/te/5843/1.html (checked 5 January 2004).

Guattari, F. and Negri A. (1990) *Communists Like Us: new spaces of liberty, new lines of alliance*, New York: Semiotext(e).

Guevara, C., Loveman, B. and Davies, T. (2002) *Guerilla Warfare*, Wilmington: Scholarly Resources.

Gunkel, D. (2001) *Hacking Cyberspace*, Boulder: Westview Press.

Gutman, E. (2002) 'Who Lost China's Internet?' *The Daily Standard*, 25 February; available at http://www.weeklystandard.com/Content/Public/Articles/000/000/000/922dgmtd.asp (checked 11 March 2002).

Hacktivismo (2003) 'Release of Six/Four'; http://www.hacktivismo.com (checked 17 October 2003).

Hafner, K. and Lyon, M. (1996) *Where Wizards Stay Up Late: the origins of the Internet*, New York: Simon and Schuster.

Handy, C. (1995) *The EmptyRaincoat: making sense of the future*, New York: Random House.

Hardt, M. and Negri, A. (2000) *Empire*, Cambridge, MA: Harvard University Press.

Harvey, N. (1998) *The Chiapas Rebellion: the struggle for land and democracy*, London: Duke University Press.

Hawn, M. (1996) 'Fear of a Hack Planet: the strange metamorphosis of the computer hacker', *The Site*, 15 July.

Hein, G. (2001) 'Microsoft.Net: a new monopoly?', *Cnet News.com*; available at http://news.com.com/2010–1078–281547.html?legacy=cnet (checked 31 January 2002).

Hencke, D. (1998) 'Whitehall Attempts to Foil Net Hackers', *Guardian Weekly*, 26 April.

Hobsbawm, E. (1988) *The Age of Capital*, London: Abacus.

Hobsbawm, E. (1989) *The Age of Empire*, London: Abacus.

Hobsbawm, E. (1995) *The Age of Extremes*, London: Abacus.

Holloway, J. and Pelaez, E. (1998) *Zapatista!: reinventing revolution in Mexico*, London: Pluto.

Jordan, J. (2003) 'The Art of Desertion', *Presentation at Live Culture: live art at the Tate Modern*, 30 March; available at http://www.tate.org.uk/audiovideo/live_culture_conference.htm (checked 23 October 2003).

Jordan, T. (1999a) *Cyberpower: the culture and politics of cyberspace and the Internet*, London: Routledge.

Jordan, T. (1999b) 'New Space, New Politics?: cyberpolitics and the Electronic Frontier Foundation', in Jordan, T. and Lent, A. (eds) *Storming the Millennium: the new politics of change*, London: Lawrence and Wishart: 80–107.

Jordan, T. (2002) *Activism!: direct action, hacktivism and the future of society*, London: Reaktion.

Jordan, T. and Lent, A. (eds) (1999) *Storming the Millennium: the new politics of change*, London: Lawrence and Wishart.

Jordan, T. and Taylor, P. (1998) 'A Sociology of Hackers', *Sociological Review* 46 (4): 757–80.

Kane, P. (1989) *V.I.R.U.S. Protection: Vital Information Resources Under Siege*, New York: Bantam.

Karasic, C. (2001) Email interview conducted by Paul A. Taylor, September.

Klein, N. (2000) *No Logo*, New York: Flamingo.

Lash, S. (2002) *Critique of Information*, London: Sage.

Lasn, K. (1999) *Culture Jam: the uncooling of America*, New York: HarperCollins.

Latour, B. (1988) 'The Prince for Machines as Well as for Machinations', in Elliott, B. (ed.) *Technology and Social Process*, Edinburgh: Edinburgh University Press: 20–43.

Leadbetter, C. (1999) *Living on Thin Air: the new economy*, London: Penguin.

Lefebvre, H. (1991) *The Production of Space*, Oxford: Blackwell.

Levy, S. (1984) *Hackers: heroes of the computer revolution*, New York: Bantam Doubleday Dell.

Lynch, D. (2000) 'Wired Women: it's a guy thing – why are there so few female hackers?' *ABCNews.com*; available at http://abcnews.go.com/sections/tech/WiredWomen/wiredwomen000223.html (accessed 4 January 2004).

McKay, G. (ed.) (1998) *DiY Culture: party and protest in nineties Britain*, London: Verso.

McIntosh, N. (2000) 'Could You Pass the Tiger Test?' *The Guardian*, 8 March.

McLuhan, M. (1964) *Understanding Media*, New York: New American Library.

Maffesoli, M. (1996) *The Time of the Tribes: the decline of individualism in mass society*, London: Sage.

Marcos (2000) *Our Word is Our Weapon: selected writings Subcomandante Marcos*, edited by Juana Ponce de León, London: Serpents Tail.

Marx, K. and Engels, F. (1972) 'Manifesto of the Communist Party', in Tucker, R. (ed.) *The Marx-Engels Reader*, second edition, New York: Norton: 469–500.

Meikle, G. (2002) *Future Active: media activism and the Internet*, London: Routledge.

Melucci, A. (1996) *The Playing Self*, Cambridge: Cambridge University Press.

Mentor, The (1986) 'The Conscience of a Hacker', *Phrack* 1(7) Phile 3; available at http://www.phrack.org (checked 5 January 2004).

Meyer, G. and Thomas, J. (1990) '(Witch)hunting for the Computer Underground: Joe McCarthy in a leisure suit', *The Critical Criminologist*, 2 September: 225–53.

Miller, L. (1995) 'Women and Children First: gender and the settling of the electronic frontier', in Boal, I. and Brooks, J. (eds) *Resisting the Virtual Life: the culture and politics of information*, San Francisco: City Lights Books: 49–57.

Moody, G. (2001) *Rebel Code: Linux and the open source revolution*, London: Penguin.

Moreiras, A. (1993) 'The Leap and the Lapse: hacking a private site in cyberspace', in Conley, V. (ed.) *Rethinking Technologies*, Minneapolis: University of Minnesota Press: 191–206.

Negroponte, N. (1995) *Being Digital*, London: Hodder and Stoughton.

New Scientist (2002) 'Web "camouflage" aims to beat censors', *New Scientist*, 22 July; available at http://www.newscientist.com/news/news.jsp?id=ns99992577 (checked 16 August 2002).

Noon, Jeff (1995) *Pollen*, Mancheser: Ringpull Press.

Petersen, J. aka Agent Steal (1997) 'Everything a Hacker Needs to Know about Getting Busted by the Feds'; available at http://www.grayarea.com/agsteal.html (checked 23 October 2003).

Pickerill, J. (2001) 'Weaving a Green Web: environmental protest and computer-mediated communication in Britain', in Webster, F. (ed.) *Culture and Politics in the Information Age: a new politics?*, London: Routledge: 142–66.

Postman, N. (1990) 'Informing Ourselves to Death', *German Informatics Society*, 11 (October); available at http://world.std.com/~jimf/informing.html (checked 9 October 2003).

Powers, R. (1998) *Gain*, London: William Heinemann.

Ravetz, J. (1996) 'The Microcybernetic Revolution and the Dialectics of Ignorance', in Sardar, Z. and Ravetz, J. (1996) *Cyberfutures: culture and politics on the Information Superhighway*, London: Pluto: 42–60.

Ronfeldt, D. and Arquilla, J. (2001a) 'Emergence and Influence of the Zapatista Netwar', in Ronfeldt, D. and Arquilla, J. (eds) *Networks and Netwars: the future of terror, crime and militancy*, Santa Monica: Rand Corporation: 177–98; available at http://www.rand.org/publications/MR/MR1382/ (checked 30 January 2002).

Ronfeldt, D. and Arquilla, J. (eds) (2001b) *Networks and Netwars: the future of terror, crime and militancy*, Santa Monica: Rand Corporation; available at http://www.rand.org/publications/MR/MR1382/ (checked 30 January 2002).

Ronfeldt, D., Arquilla, J., Fuller, G. and Fuller, M. (1998) *The Zapatista Social Netwar in Mexico*, Santa Monica: Rand; available at http://www.rand.org/publications/MR/MR994/ (checked 30 January 2002).

Ross, A. (1991) *Strange Weather*, London: Verso.

Ross, J. (2000) *The War Against Oblivion: the Zapatista chronicles*, Philadelphia: Common Courage Press.

Roszak, T. (1986) *The Cult of Information: the folklore of computers and the true art of thinking*, Cambridge: Lutterworth Press.

Rovira, G. (2000) *Women of Maize: indigenous women and the Zapatista rebellion*, London: Latin American Bureau.

Rowbotham, S., Segal, L. and Wainwright, H. (1979) *Beyond the Fragments: feminism and the making of socialism*, London: Merlin.

®™ark (1997) *A System for Change*; available at http://www.rtmark.com/docsystem.html (checked 23 October 2003).

®™ark (1998a) *Sabotage and the New World Order*; available at http://www.rtmark. com/arse.html (checked 23 October 2003).

®™ark (1998b) *Curation*; available at *http:*//www.rtmark.com/curation.html (checked 23 October 2003).

®™ark, (2000) 'Etoys Finally Drops Lawsuit, Pays Court Costs'; available at http://www.rtmark.com/etoyprtriumph.html (checked 14 October 2003).

Ruffin, O. (2000) 'Valid Campaign Tactic or Terrorist Act?: the Cult of the Dead Cow's response to client-side distributed denial-of-service'; available at http://www.gn.acp.org/pmhp/ehippies (checked 05 March 2002).

Ruffin, O. (2002) 'Peekabooty Update: press release'; available at www.cultdeadcow. com (checked 05 March 2002).

Rushkoff, D. (1994) *Cyberia: life in the trenches of hyberspace*, San Franciso: HarperSanFrancisco.

Sardar, Z. and Ravetz, J. (1996) *Cyberfutures: culture and politics on the Information Superhighway*, London: Pluto.

Schlosser, E. (2001) *Fast Food Nation: what the all-American meal is doing to the world*, London: Penguin.

Segan, S. (2000a) 'Part 1: hacker women are few but strong'; available at http://abcnews.go.com/sections/tech/DailyNews/hackerwomen000602.html#top (accessed 4 January 2004).

Segan, S. (2000b) 'Part 2: female hackers face challenges'; available at http:// abcnews.go.com/sections/tech/DailyNews/hackerwomen000609.html (accessed 4 January 2004).

Shachtman, N. (2002) 'A New Code for Anonymous Web Use'; available at http://www.wired.com/news/privacy/0,1848,53799,00.html (checked 16 August 2002).

Shimomura, T. (1995) *Takedown,* with John Markoff, New York: Secker and Warburg.

Smith, G. (1999) 'Future Schlock', excerpted from *Foreign Policy Magazine*; available at http://www.soci.niu.edu/~crypt/other/fpschlok.htm (checked 23 October 2003).

Starr, A. (2000) *Naming the Enemy: anti-corporate movements confront globalization*, London: Zed Books.

Stephenson, N. (1992) *Snow Crash*, New York: RoC.

Taylor, P. (1999) *Hackers: crime in the digital sublime*, London: Routledge.

Tomlinson, J. (1999) *Globalization and Culture*, Cambridge: Polity.

Touraine, A. (2002) 'The Importance of Social Movements', *Social Movement Studies* 1(1): 89–96.

Tucker, R. (ed.) (1978) *The Marx-Engels Reader*, second edition, New York: Norton.

Turkle, S. (1978) *Psychoanalytic Politics: Freud's French Revolution*, Cambridge, MA: MIT Press.

Turkle, S. (1984) *The Second Self: computers and the human spirit*, London: Granada.

Ullman, E. (1997) *Close to the Machine: technophilia and its discontents*, San Francisco: City Lights Books.

Vallee, J. (1984) *The Network Revolution: confessions of a computer scientist*, London: Penguin.

Virus Bulletin (1998a) 'Virus Bulletin', September: 4.

Virus Bulletin (1998b) 'Virus Bulletin', October: 4.

Wark, M. (1992) 'Cyberpunk: from subculture to mainstream'; available at http://www.dmc.mq.edu.au/mwark/warchive/21*C/21c-cyberpunk.html (checked 21 October 2003).

Webster, F. (ed.) (2001) *Culture and Politics in the Information Age: a new politics?*, London: Routledge.

Weinberg, B. (2000) *Homage to Chiapas: the new indigenous struggles in Mexico*, London: Verso.

Weizenbaum, J. (1976) *Computer Power and Human Reason: from judgement to calculation*, New York: W. H. Freeman.

Wishart, A. and Boschler, R. (2002) *Leaving Reality Behind: the battle for the soul of the Internet*, London: Fourth Estate.

Wray, S. (1998) 'World Wide Web of Hacktivism: a mapping of extra-parliamentarian direct action net politics', a paper for the World Wide Web and Contemporary Cultural Theory conference, Drake University; available at http://www.nyu.edu/projects/wray/ecd.html (checked 29 January 2002).

Wright, S. (2002) *Storming Heaven: class composition and struggle in Italian Autonomist Marxism*, London: Pluto.

Index